HURON COUNTY

W9-CPP-268

HURON COUNTY LIBRARY

2 008 203618 5

ST. LAWRENCE ISLANDS
NATIONAL PARK

GARDEN OF THE GREAT SPIRIT

An Indian legend tells of two powerful gods, one good and the other evil, who argued fiercely over which one of them would rule the land and the mighty St. Lawrence River. The argument became an earth-shaking combat when each tore huge handfuls of rock from the face of the earth to heave furiously across the river at the other. A great many fistfuls were thrown, most of which fell short of their target to land in and about the river. Finally, good triumphed, and evil spirits were forever banished from the land. Under an enchanted spell, forests flourished on the thousand chunks of rugged rock which had fallen into the river. The rocks became the Thousand Islands: Manitouana, the Garden of the Great Spirit.

CLINTON
PUBLIC LIBRARY

ST. LAWRENCE
ISLANDS
NATIONAL PARK

DON ROSS

Douglas & McIntyre
Vancouver/Toronto

In association with Parks Canada

JUN 23 '87

91302

Copyright © Minister of Supply and Services Canada, 1983
Catalogue No. R62-150-1-1983E

All rights reserved. No part of this book may be reproduced or
transmitted in any form by any means without permission
in writing from the publisher, except by a reviewer,
who may quote brief passages in a review.

Douglas & McIntyre Ltd., 1615 Venables Street, Vancouver,
British Columbia V5L 2H1

Canadian Cataloguing in Publication Data

Ross, Don.
    St. Lawrence Islands National Park

    Bibliography: p.
    ISBN 0-88894-379-2

    1. St. Lawrence Islands National Park (Ont.) –
    Description and travel – Guide-books. 2. Thousand
    Islands Region (Ont.) – History. 3. Zoology –
    Ontario – Thousand Islands Region. I. Parks Canada.
    II. Title.
    FC3064.S4R67   917.13'7   C83-091127-8
    F1059.S4R67

Design: Barbara Hodgson
Printed and bound in Canada by D.W. Friesen & Sons Ltd.

 Parks   Parcs
Canada Canada

CONTENTS

We left Kingston for Montreal on the tenth of May, at half-past nine in the evening, and proceeded in a steamboat down the St. Lawrence River. The beauty of this noble stream at almost any point, but especially in the commencement of this journey, when it winds its way among the Thousand Islands, can hardly be imagined. The number and constant succession of these islands, all green and richly wooded; their fluctuating sizes, some so large that for half an hour together one among them will appear as the opposite bank of the river, and some so small that they are mere dimples on its broad bosom; their infinite variety of shapes; and the numberless combinations of beautiful forms which trees growing on them present: all form a picture fraught with uncommon interest and pleasure.''

Charles Dickens in *American Notes*, from an excursion through the Thousand Islands in the early 1840s.

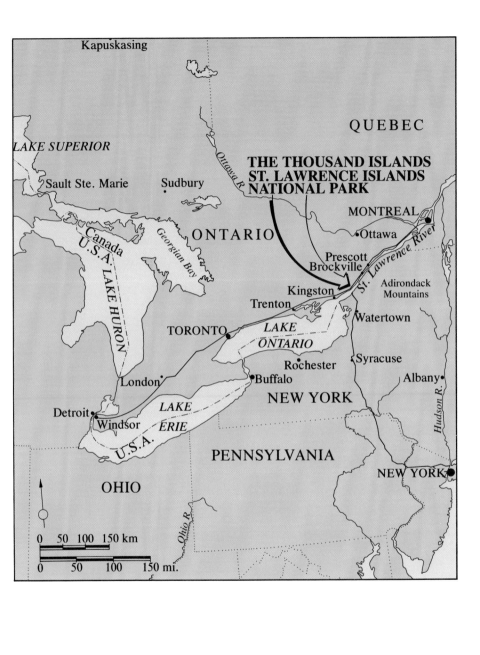

Kapuskasing

QUEBEC

LAKE SUPERIOR

**THE THOUSAND ISLANDS
ST. LAWRENCE ISLANDS
NATIONAL PARK**

Sault Ste. Marie Sudbury

MONTREAL

ONTARIO •Ottawa

Canada
U.S.A.

Georgian Bay

St. Lawrence River

Prescott
Brockville

Adirondack
Mountains

*LAKE
HURON*

Kingston

Trenton

Watertown

TORONTO

*LAKE
ONTARIO*

London Rochester Syracuse

Buffalo

Albany•

Detroit• **NEW YORK**

Windsor

*LAKE
ERIE*

U.S.A.

Hudson R.

PENNSYLVANIA

NEW YORK

OHIO

Ottawa R.

Ohio R.

0 50 100 150 km.

0 50 100 150 mi.

INTRODUCTION

*To protect for all time those places which are
significant examples of Canada's natural
and cultural heritage and also to encourage
public understanding, appreciation, and
enjoyment of this heritage in ways which leave
it unimpaired for future generations.*
Parks Canada mandate

The idea to preserve natural landscapes and heritage landmarks in a national system of parks was born at a time when much of Canada had not yet been completely mapped. It began in 1885 when a mineral hot springs and the beautiful land surrounding it at Sulphur Mountain, Alberta, was reserved by the government of Canada as a public park. The 16-km^2 reserve became the core of Banff National Park, Canada's first. The National Park system continues to protect superb examples of our country's natural landscape. Parks are found in every part of Canada, from Terra Nova in Newfoundland to Pacific Rim on Vancouver Island, British Columbia, and from Canada's most southerly mainland at Point Pelee, Ontario, to Auyuittuq National Park on Baffin Island inside the Arctic Circle. The system would be complete if each of the thirty-nine terrestrial and nine marine natural regions in Canada were represented by national parks; to date, there are twenty-nine such parks, at least one in each province and territory.

Places, people, events and achievements that have marked the progress of Canada as a growing nation are commemorated as National Historic Parks and Sites. This wide-ranging system preserves such sites as a Viking settlement at L'anse aux Meadows, Newfoundland, the reconstruction of the Fortress of Louisbourg in Nova Scotia, and the re-creation of the exciting gold rush setting at Dawson City in the Yukon. Also commemorated are many heritage buildings, canals and rivers as well as certain lands and waterways set aside for recreation and conservation. The responsibility for ensuring that these special places and achievements will not be lost to future generations in our country has been given to Parks Canada, part of Environment Canada.

When it was established in 1904, St. Lawrence Islands became the fifth oldest National Park in Canada. This smallest of national parks is, in a sense, a sample of the Thousand Islands; it includes portions of mainland and several islands in the region of the upper St. Lawrence River between Kingston and Brockville. Despite its small size, the park is extremely rich in natural and cultural history features. There are three other Parks Canada sites of note within a short distance of St. Lawrence Islands National Park. Fort Wellington National Historic Park at Prescott, a large blockhouse fortification and military convoy staging area on the river, played an active role in the defence of Canada in the first half of the nineteenth century. The Rideau Canal, between Kingston and Ottawa on the combined routes of the Cataraqui and Rideau rivers, was completed in 1832 as a military and trade route to bypass the less easily defended waterway of the St. Lawrence River. The canal's lock system still functions as a recreational route: many of the original buildings at the lock stations have been restored and opened to help tell the canal's story to visitors. In Kingston, Bellevue House National Historic Park and its grounds have been restored to the period when John A. Macdonald, who would become Canada's first prime minister, lived there with his family.

A visit to all four of these Parks Canada locations in eastern Ontario provides insight into the environment, life and times of this long-settled area of Canada.

There are two main sections to this book. The first highlights the natural and cultural heritage of St. Lawrence Islands National Park. The second is designed to aid those who may wish to become acquainted with it at first hand. Whether used as introduction or souvenir, the book's purpose will have been served if it helps guide the reader to an appreciation and active concern for this remarkable region.

Wave-washed rock, Thwartway Island

THE FACE
OF THE LAND

The finest workers in stone are not copper or
steel tools, but the gentle touches of air
and water working at their leisure with a liberal
allowance of time.
Henry David Thoreau

Time, patient and enduring, frowns from each weathering precipice of the Thousand Islands. Run a hand over the rock. Feel the gentle rasp of dull-edged crystals. Ancient granite, ruggedly beautiful with the marks of time, forms the fundamental substance and character of this land.

There is probably no place where the complex geological story of the Thousand Islands can be deduced as well as among the islands and channels of the Ivy Lea area. Here is the centre of the Frontenac Arch, a structure born of the earth's dynamic forces: the bowed

granite spine of a mountain chain so ancient that its rock has endured a quarter of the earth's long history. Buried under seafloor sediments, exhumed and scoured in four glacial ages, and flooded as an outlet to the greatest reservoir of fresh water in the world, the Thousand Islands region now stolidly resists the wear of the elements and bears the transient expressions of nature on its subtly serene surface. Even with the passage of so much time, there are still excellent clues on the face of the land to help us piece the story together.

Granite cliffs near Thousand Islands Bridge

11

ORIGINS

Since the moment of its origin, forces in the earth have never been at rest. The upper crust of the planet, which cradles the oceans and is the land surface of our world, is adrift on its molten inner layers. Through the more than four billion years of the earth's history, continents have shifted, oceans have changed shape and depth, and mountain ranges have come and gone. Such monumental events happen so slowly that the drift of continents was not proven and measured until recent years. Only occasional violent upheavals such as earthquakes and volcanic eruptions reveal the unyielding stresses beneath us.

One-and-a-half billion years ago, whatever landform existed in this area of the world was erased. So dramatic were the geological events that no trace of any of the previous structures remain. A vast area south of the already ancient Canadian Shield sagged deep below sea level and was flooded by the then lifeless seas for hundreds of millions of years. Rivers brought the silt of eroding landscapes to settle in the quiet depths. Layer upon layer of sediment collected until its very thickness created a crushing weight. In time, pressure and the heat generated by it compressed the sediments into sedimentary rock. Eventually, the bottommost layer of sandstone greatly changed in form to become finely banded, almost crystalline, rock. The sagging crust finally gave way under the tremendous burden. Ever so slowly, the layered rock was heaved, bent and cracked. Molten rock from deep in the earth forced upwards into the fractures. Mountains rose from the depths of the sea. The molten rock and the radically heat-changed layered rock just above it cooled slowly at the roots of the mountains to become the various granites and gneisses. In shifting and settling, new fractures shot through the formations, and igneous (fire-formed) rocks were squeezed into them. These structures are called dykes, if they run vertically, or sills, if they are horizontal. One such dyke, of very fine, dark crystals, is exposed in a frost-shattered cliff face at the beginning of the hiking trail at Mallorytown Landing.

The granite rocks contain orthoclase (white) and plagioclase (pink) feldspars, quartz, hornblende, pyroxene, and biotite mica in various proportions. A distinctive granite of the Thousand Islands, pink in colour, with medium-sized crystals, is called Rockport granite and is rich in biotite. Rockport granite forms much of Hill Island, the Rockport-to-Landon's Bay area as well as the Navy Fleet, Lake Fleet and Admiralty islands. Migmatite is a mixture of granitic and metamorphic (heat- and pressure-changed) gneisses forming much of the mainland east of Rockport along with Grenadier and its associated islands.

12

The ancient mountains in this area finished building some 600 to 800 million years ago. They were eroding at their summits and flanks even as they were lifted and folded skyward. Erosion, while seldom dramatic, is just as irresistible as the powerful building forces of the earth. No mountain range on earth has withstood the weathering of the ages: even the young Rocky Mountains will someday be reduced to rolling hills. As the building slowed then ceased, agents of weathering brought all materials of those soaring heights to a lowest level. Wind and water, freeze and thaw slowly chipped, abraded and broke particles free, nudging them ever downhill to eventual destinations in the depths of the sea. The mountains here were almost entirely reduced. Their fragments would become recycled as building blocks elsewhere, at another time.

As the mountains eroded, their roots gradually floated upwards in a process called "isostasy." About 500 million years ago, the ancient mountain roots rose to daylight. The landform then would have looked very much as we see it today, except that its surface had not yet been polished by glaciers.

Some 450 to 500 million years ago the earth's surface again shifted and sagged. The ocean once more flooded the land, and just as hundreds of millions of years before, sediments settled to the sea floor so that layer built on layer. The mountain roots were in time buried under sedimentary rock. This time, however, the deposits did not become deep enough to subject the new rock to the kind of enormous stress that would have radically altered its form.

At the beginning of this long period of flooding, the water was quite shallow. The earliest layers of sediment settled in the valleys between the great hills. These were probably wind-deposited dune sands which were eroded into the coastal waters to become shallow marine deposits. Primitive worms foraged in the sandy shallows; their tunnels and microscopic mouth parts are still preserved in the rock as a record of some of the earliest complex animal life on earth. The worms distorted much of the fine detail of the sands. Even so, occasional ripple marks, like those formed by small waves at a beach edge today, were buried intact under settling silt. An example of this phenomenon is revealed on the shores of Gordon Island where the layered rock has broken partially away. This oldest sandstone is called the Potsdam Formation, named for the location in New York state where it was first described.

B etween the upper, younger layers of Potsdam sandstone, called the Nepean Formation, and the granite there is often found a conglomerate rock — a rock that looks like rounded stones of all sizes in a fine-grained cement. Such conglomerates, as seen at Brown's Bay and on Hill Island, look at a glance as if they were a fossilized, gravelly soil.

Above the fine-grained, silica-rich Nepean Formation are the blue-grey and yellow March Formation sandstones, composed of quartz sand, with calcium-rich mud and organic material from deposits in shallow water. Both the Nepean and March sandstones lie mainly to the east of the Thousand Islands, as do somewhat younger limestone dolomites (limestone with magnesium carbonate) of the Oxford Formation. Fossil algae and primitive shellfish in this last formation tell of the warm shallow seas that then lay upon the land.

To the west of the Thousand Islands, as at the south tip of Cedar Island of the national park and in the Fort Henry hillside, are very old limestones of the Gull River Formation. These are the youngest of the rocks found in islands, and are roughly 450 million years of age.

Sandstone bluffs, Gordon Island

14

Wave-worn limestone, Cedar Island

Folded gneiss and granite, Mulcaster Island

Close-up of polished granite

About the same time that the sandstone-creating seas lay upon the land, a slow uplift of the old mountain roots took place. A gentle arch—the Frontenac Arch—was formed, its axis running southeast from the Madawaska region to the Adirondack Mountains. Although the uplift halted hundreds of millions of years ago, the granite of the Frontenac Arch remains as the backbone of south-central Canada and divides the otherwise level plains of southern Ontario.

During the long erosion of the sedimentary rocks, fragments of sand and silt were trapped in valleys. Eventually the soil was enriched by the decay of plant life, and in time, the landscape came vibrantly alive.

THE ICE AGES

Finally, just a million years ago, the last major events to shape the Thousand Islands occurred. Although the reasons for the four successive ice ages are not fully understood, there is no argument that they were profoundly significant for most of Canada. The surface character of the landscape—the soils and streams, the lakes and living land—was erased by the powerful ice sheets.

In the Thousand Islands, the direction of ice flow seems to have been guided by topography. The old mountain chain roots may have been unearthed by the first ice sheets, when the limestone and sandstone veneer was peeled away over the Frontenac Arch. In later advances, the rock- and gravel-laden ice sculpted the granite to the shapes we know today.

Northeast facing slopes bore the brunt of the gouging, bulldozing ice advance to become rounded and polished. The fine detail of the glacier's torturous passage is recorded on the bald, smooth rock. Chatter marks are crescent-shaped pits in the surface where boulders jammed against the rock, broke free, jammed, and broke free again. Striations and grooves, some narrow lines and some broadly U-shaped, mark where rock was dragged along. Westerly slopes are often clifflike and broken where the ice found weaknesses and plucked away the looser rock.

The glacier was a mammoth, slow-moving flood of ice, and just as a flood carries sediment, the glacier too was enormously burdened. At its maximum, the last ice sheet was about 2 to 3 km deep over this area. The quantity of mud, gravel, rock, sand, earth and tree trunks carried in it was staggering. When the ice melted, that load dropped out. Although this debris was generally left unsorted, flowing melt-water at ice front occasionally created features of layered sand and various sizes of stones called kames, as on Hill Island and in the Ivy

Lea area. Streams running under or through the ice left meandering gravel ridges called eskers. One such esker runs the length of Grenadier Island, linking what would otherwise be individual low-lying granite islands.

The land sank beneath the weight of the continental ice sheets but began a slow rise to its present level when the ice melted. Although a major river system existed before the ice ages where the Great Lakes now lie, the lakes themselves came into being when glaciers gouged huge basins along the rivers' channels.

About 12,000 years ago, the Thousand Islands were flooded by the ocean for a brief period. The land still sagged from the weight of the ice, and the ocean level rose, replenished by meltwater. By 11,500 years ago, the St. Lawrence was firmly established as the outlet of the Great Lakes.

THE ST. LAWRENCE RIVER

At the end of the last ice age, the St. Lawrence River slowly took its present course. An early stage of Lake Ontario lay west of the island chain which runs from Prince Edward County to the American shore. The lake poured over a sill between Main Duck and the Galloo islands, about 40 km south of Kingston. This early channel for the St. Lawrence River cut into the lake bed from that sill and along the south side of Grindstone Island. A more powerful river flowed from the upper Great Lakes down the Trent-Severn corridor to enter the Thousand Islands north of Grindstone Island. Both of these young rivers flooded through the hills of the old granite mountain roots, carrying away glacial debris and clays along their new course. At the crest of the Frontenac Arch in the heart of the Thousand Islands, the rivers poured over ridges of rock, plunging down as rapids and waterfalls to cut deep pools below. The rivers finally merged at the foot of Hill and Wellesley islands to end their journey in an inland arm of the Atlantic Ocean, the Champlain Sea, not far beyond. Today's turbulent waters in the channels at Georgina Island and just above Alexandria Bay, New York, mark where the old rivers tumbled over the now submerged rapids and sill. It is here that Lake Ontario begins its seaward race.

At the southeast end of Bostwick Island in the Admiralty Group near Gananoque is a bay with a unique geological origin. Halfmoon Bay was created in a rushing torrent of waters perhaps as long ago as a half billion years. Water poured over the Thousand Islands, which were probably submerged at the time, and shot through a cut at the end of the bay. Whirlpools and eddies formed, spinning rocks and stones as if they were sand grains swirled in the bottom of a glass. The abrasive action of stone on stone wore away the rock walls near the back of the bay, leaving a broadly scalloped pattern. Still farther back are two huge cauldron-like holes in the rock, called potholes, also carved by the whirling eddies. At a later time, this entire area became covered with sedimentary rock, and the potholes were filled in. Then, during the last ice ages, the softer rock was scraped away. Finally, meltwaters of the ice sheets raced through the back of the bay, exposing, scouring and polishing the old potholes once again. The potholes collect rainwater, leaves and twigs. A green frog lives in one of them.

Halfmoon Bay potholes

CLIMATE

If we are especially aware of any aspect of our environment, it is the weather. It affects our activities and our moods and even our economy. Since weather is a demonstration of the atmosphere's unsettled character, it is not surprising that changes in it frequently catch us off guard. A seventeenth-century traveller's account speaks for the many boaters in the Thousand Islands who fail to notice the changing sky to the west.

Capt. Basil Hall and his family were en route from Kingston to Montreal by batteau on 8 August 1827 when he wrote:

> Nothing could be more prosperous than the first part of our passage, and we skimmed merrily along, with the stream in our favour, amongst the Thousand Islands, as they were called, with a brisk wind, also, to help the current.
> Towards sunset, the sky became suddenly overcast by a thunder-cloud, upon which the Voyageurs, as these boat men are called, held a

Lifting fog

council of war, in a corrupted, or perhaps antiquated, sort of French, of which I understood very few words; the result was, the expediency of rowing into a nook, or cove, where a little brook escaped from the woods, and leaped into the St. Lawrence.

Hall, despite his naval background, did not see why the rivermen wanted to put ashore. After all, they had a canvas shelter called a hurricane-house over the batteau, so he insisted that they continue downstream.

We had not gone 150 yards, however, before the thunder-cloud broke close to us, with such a peal as I have seldom heard; and I was fain to make the amende honorable, by acknowledging my ignorance, and confessing that I had done wrong in despising the recommendation of such experienced guides. I begged them to row back again as hard as they could, which they did with great cheerfulness, and with the characteristic politeness of all who speak their language, without the slightest show of triumph or reproach. But, before we got to the landing place, there came on a show of hailstones, as big as nuts, by which we were so finely pelted for our obstinacy, that we thought ourselves fortunate to find shelter in an old cowshed.

As quick as the summer squall had come, it was over. The party left the shed to make its way up a path along La Rue creek. By the light of the moon in the clear sky, they came to the house of Billa La Rue, where they spent the rest of the night.

In the short term, weather systems in the Thousand Islands are moderately predictable. The Great Lakes basin lies between Pacific Ocean and Gulf of Mexico sources of warm, moist air. The Arctic regions of northern Canada are sources of cold, dry air. The air masses become distorted while travelling across the continent over such varied terrain as mountains, prairie, uplands and lake districts. These constant changes and the force of one air mass against the other cause the variations in approaching weather systems that keep the weatherman on the defensive. Although low pressure air masses originate elsewhere, most leave the continent by way of the St. Lawrence River valley.

Those who know the Thousand Islands region agree that one of its most marvellous features is a moderate climate and four distinct and enjoyable seasons. Much of the climate's character is due to the presence of the Great Lakes, especially Lake Ontario. Water warms and cools more slowly than air, and so the lake and river help check temperature extremes. In ice-free seasons, the great quantity of water moderates the air temperatures along the shores. Frost hazard is reduced and the growing season is extended. Trees leaf out and flowers bloom earlier; fall colour peaks noticeably later. In summer, temperatures seldom reach extreme degrees and nights are pleasantly cool. In winter, before the January freeze-up, winds off the lake and river make for milder days relative to adjacent inland regions. These moisture-laden winds blowing off the water over the cooler land also often create snowstorms. The effects of Lake Ontario are extended eastward by the prevailing southwest winds which carry the lake-moderated weather along the St. Lawrence River valley.

The sunniest, most cloud-free period in the Thousand Islands is July and August; November and December get the award for being the dreariest months since skies are overcast more than half the time. Fog is common during these same grey months, when moist air rapidly cools over the river's surface. In the heart of the Thousand Islands, the first frost is expected around 10 October and the last frost around 1 May. By the first of December the area will probably receive its first significant snowfall, and the heaviest snows can be expected in December, January and February, with accumulations of 40 to 50 cm per month. The snow cover remains an average of 100 days, with a slightly greater accumulation at the area's east end.

Early in December, shallow bays and inlets begin to freeze and by the end of the month they are icebound. During the entire period of freeze-up, however, there are few places where the ice is completely reliable, for insulating snow cover and current eddies continually counter ice formation. Ducks and even the occasional eagle gather at these few spots where fishing is still possible. The turbulent fast waters in the main channels at Ivy Lea, Brockville and Alexandria Bay generally prevent freeze-up and by late March, most of the river will be free of ice.

The presence of the lake of course increases humidity. Compared to the hinterland, the humidity in the islands in an average year is 15 percent higher. In early spring, fall and early winter, there is greater cloud development over the water than over the land, but this effect is reversed in summer. However, in the warm months, the lake water cools the lowest air layers, thereby reducing the frequency of summer showers and thunderstorms. Boaters who come from farther west along Lakes Ontario and Erie are accustomed to a thorough thrashing when awesome midsummer thunderheads develop. Here, however, they are usually relieved to find themselves with a ringside seat at storms which do not develop over the St. Lawrence but rage a few kilometres north or south of the river.

All in all, Lake Ontario's effect on the climate of the Thousand Islands area is of great importance to natural communities. The frost-free period is a case in point. At the west end of the area, there are about 160 days without frost. Towards the east end, at Stovin Island and Brockville, the period is reduced to 143 days. This trend

Tom Thumb Island in winter

continues downriver until the effect of the lake is no longer felt. At Cornwall, there are about 120 frost-free days, roughly comparable to the Ottawa region and to Gouverneur, New York, which is 35 km south of Brockville. Consequently, trees leaf out and spring flowers bloom slightly later along the river than just a few kilometres inland. Fall colour in the islands is at its peak noticeably later than inland. A boundary between two plant hardiness zones lies just west of Brockville, reflecting a change in susceptibility to frost damage to more southerly plants.

Monthly precipitation varies from a low near 70 mm in February, March and April to a high of 92 mm in November. This unusual trend where fall precipitation exceeds that of spring is due to late fall lake-effect storms and snowshowers, when moisture-laden winds sweep down the broad river valley. May has more rainy days than any other month. June through September see an average of nine days of rain per month. Thunderstorms occur mainly in June, July and August with the greatest frequency in July.

Although westerly winds prevail, winds from every point of the compass have been recorded. Low and high pressure zones are much more intense and move more rapidly in winter than in summer. Strong summer winds are rare and are felt only with exceptional weather systems, thunderstorms and squall lines. When these do hit, however, hang onto your hat and take a reef in your mainsail. Winds average 15 to 18 km/h from the southwest about half the year, with

Hemlock stand

speeds of 8 to 10 km/h the usual summer fare. Being generally sun-powered, the fair weather winds are often lightest in the morning, peaking in midafternoon and diminishing by dusk.

Microclimate

No discussion on the climate of the Thousand Islands would be complete without mention of a phenomenon called "microclimate" —small but consistent variations over short distances in temperature, humidity, rate of evaporation, exposure to wind and to sunlight. In the Thousand Islands this effect is created by the rugged landscape: the climate on open, south-facing slopes is measurably different from that at sheltered, north-facing slopes. For example, the evaporation rate of water in a rocky, open pitch-pine stand on a southwest point may be 500 percent greater than in a shady hemlock stand on the north shore of the same island. Daytime temperature will be consistently higher as well. As will be seen in the next section, when conditions vary in the physical environment, there will be a greater variety of life in the natural communities. Microclimate is a key factor in maintaining the diversity of life in this region.

THE LIVING COMMUNITY

First light found the hunter motionless, his back to the sun, beneath the overhang of willows on the island's sandy north shore. Morning mists began their lazy swirl in the breath of the sun-born breeze. A loon materialized from the mist, now casually alert to the sky above, now, head submerged, attentive to the possibility of breakfast below. It slipped beneath the quiet surface, chasing a school of silvery prey shoreward, and emerged satisfied. This seemed a good omen to the hunter.

He tensed. The elk that he knew was on the island browsed her way to the shore. This had to be the place she would come to drink; low cliffs rimmed the remainder of the island. The moment came. The lance flew. But no! She started at his move, and the lance flashed past its mark to rattle on the stones beyond. The sound! He knew it, and his grief was not for the animal that escaped to the aspen grove, for there would be other chances in this rich land. His prized hunting point was shattered, and there was none of the right rock in this land to replace it. He returned to the campsite, broken lance and fragment in hand, and other plans formed. He remembered the loon in the offshore shallows. Where there are little fish, there are bigger fish . . .

Although this scene is speculation, the landscape and artifacts are real. We know a man came to Gordon Island as long as 9000 years ago, and that a broken, wedge-shaped fragment of a flint hunting point was found near a sandy shore. That man's presence should be detected after so much time is due in part to fortune and in part to expert archaeological work. This find has profound significance to those tracing the development of the Thousand Islands landscape. It shows

24

that man was here not very long after the last ice age and so was a part of the region's ecology from near the outset of its greening. Obviously, the story of man cannot be separated from the story of the land.

THOUSAND ISLANDS ECOLOGY

The wildlife and plant life of the Thousand Islands appears amazingly rich and complex, but most intriguing is the number of species here that are usually more common in neighbouring forest regions. Botanist Roland Beschel has coined the term "tension zone ecology" for the Thousand Islands, where plants and animals found in several forest regions and geographic areas are intermixed. Several species are rare in the region, or in Canada, and many are at the limits of their normal distribution.

In textbook terms, the Thousand Islands falls into the Huron-Ontario section of the Great Lakes–St. Lawrence Forest Region, one of nine major forest regions in Canada. This section is typified by sugar maple and American beech woodlands, along with basswood, red and white ash, yellow birch, red maple, eastern hemlock, white pine, and red, white and bur oak trees. Other trees scattered in the woodlands are butternut, bitternut hickory, ironwood and black cherry. Plants such as red and white trillium, early meadow rue, false Solomon's seal, Canada mayflower, trout-lily and spring beauty are standard adornment on the forest floor. This forest region has often been referred to as a broad south-to-north transitional zone.

The southern forest influence can be seen from ground level to tree tops. Shagbark hickory, black maple, swamp white oak, silver maple, slippery elm, and bitternut hickory are southern trees scattered through the Thousand Islands. Winged sumac, fragrant sumac, summer grape, and southern arrow-wood are shrubs and vines at their northern limits here. Five of nine Canadian locations for winged sumac are in the area. Deerberry, Canada's rarest shrub, is known in this country only from the west end of Grenadier Island in the national park and a few plants in the Niagara Peninsula. Numerous southern plants grace woodland and field: rue anemone, round-leafed tick trefoil, pokeweed, hog peanut, bur cucumber, and giant hyssop name a few. Over 5 percent of the area's vascular plants are listed as rare in Ontario.

For northern flavour, a few boreal plants nearing the southern end of their range here are one-flowered cancer root, buffalo berry, shrubby cinquefoil, hoary willow, shining willow and ground cedar. Some trees with a northern affinity are balsam poplar, balsam fir, speckled alder, and striped maple.

Of course, a north-south transition is not unique to the Thousand

Sweet grass

Shrubby cinquefoil

Rue anemone

Islands. Temperature and day-length variations are found the world over, so that such a transition exists in every area. What is of interest are the places where normal range limits are exceeded to an unusual degree and in an unusual number of cases. In the Thousand Islands, there are many coincidences of northern and southern range limits being met, indicating that more than just climate factors are at play. Further clues to the region's tension zone ecology come from a look at east and west influences in the plant communities. Plants that hint at a more westerly origin are the tall blue joint grass. Bur oak and Manitoba maple are trees of the midwest which have extended their ranges east to this area. Notables from the more easterly Acadian Forest are grey birch, which has a western range limit near Gananoque, and red spruce, found here and sporadically in eastern Ontario. Of very special interest too are plants with coastal and Appalachian connections—pitch pine, Canadian serviceberry, whorled woodland aster, and panicled hawkeed.

A close look at the whole ecological spectrum of the Thousand Islands reveals seven interrelated explanations for its diversity.

1   The islands lie at the junction of various post-ice-age plant and animal colonization routes. Since large water bodies are barriers to the movements of most wildlife, it is natural that the islands became stepping stones around the east end of Lake Ontario and across the St. Lawrence River. As well, the shores of the young Great Lakes were like open plains when the flood of meltwater from the glaciers drained away. They became east-west corridors for the living things that arrived to colonize the new land. The shores of the Champlain Sea and then the St. Lawrence River valley, together with the Hudson River–Lake Champlain valley, were also entrance routes.

2   Lifting through the sandstone and limestone lowlands of eastern Ontario and northern New York, the granite of the Frontenac Arch marks a dramatic change in bedrock structure and soil chemistry. The more acid condition of this shield environment contrasts with the more alkaline soils of the lowlands, limiting some plants and animals and favouring others.

3   Soil formation on acid soils begins slowly, and the uneven landscape in this region further hinders the process. Soil erodes quickly from the smooth, rocky domes and either collects in rather poorly drained valleys or washes directly into the river. Consequently, since large areas of good soils seldom occur, opportunities for large forest stands are limited. Forests are found in valleys and on slopes, with one stand separated from the next by rocky ridges.

4 Lake Ontario is certainly a key factor in maintaining the southern character in the Thousand Islands. As we have seen, the lake is an enormous heat sink, cooling summer air, warming it in winter, raising humidity, and dampening daily temperature extremes year round.

5 Microclimates—those small but distinct local variations in climate patterns due primarily to the rugged landscape—account for many subtle variations throughout the Thousand Islands, thereby creating countless opportunities for animal and plant life.

6 The distance to other forest regions is relatively short, and so there is a good chance that plants or animals from the other regions can find their way here. Dramatic changes in climate conditions, for example, could encourage or discourage the survival of some plants or animals in the area. The warming trend that defeated the last ice age continued until some 3000 to 4000 years ago, and average annual temperatures then exceeded those of today by about 5°C. The southern forests advanced farther to the north, a move that was reversed when the climate again began to cool. It is possibly through such changes that the pitch pine and deerberry came to have isolated, remnant populations in the region. They continue to survive because of favourable local conditions.

7 Humans also had a hand in fashioning the pattern of living communities. A few plants are thought to have been brought in by native peoples. These include sweet grass for basket making, wild onion and mayapple for food, and bladdernut trees with their rattlelike seed pods. More sweeping changes have come about in the last three centuries as some species were selectively cut or harvested, when weeds or ornamentals were successfully introduced, and when extensive areas of countryside were altered by new land uses.

IN SEARCH OF THE TYPICAL ISLAND

Actually, the truly typical island does exist. Geologically, ecologically, climatolc cally, topographically, hydrographically and even scenically, each island is unique. Nonetheless, there is a similarity from island to island in the character of the forest. It was summarized by Roland Beschel in a study done for Parks Canada:

A generalized island is covered on its southwestern end with an open pitch pine stand. Along the shores this is replaced first by white pines, and on the northeastern end finally by hemlocks. Within this fringe of softwoods, the forest is dominated by hardwoods. Basswood is more frequent on the steeper and lower slopes, while white oak and shagbark hickory grow more towards the top of the island and red oak ranges throughout. On higher ridges, the pitch pines may extend to the top and are in turn surrounded by a band of white oak forest.

A "typical" island

Tour boat in Raft Narrows

WILDLIFE

Many boaters have seen gray squirrels swimming from island to island. It is not unusual for a squirrel to scramble up a paddle right into a boat and hitchhike to shore. Of course, squirrels don't go around highjacking yachts to go island hopping. It's just that many islands are not far apart, and perhaps the acorns look bigger on the other side of the channel. Raccoons, weasels and deer are also frequent year-round island-hoppers. Channels become even less of a barrier in winter when foxes, coyotes, voles, short-tailed shrews and porcupines use the ice to reach other islands in their search for food. In a very real sense, the islands are not isolated. In ecological terms, they are merely extensions of mainland natural communities. The size of the islands limits food supplies and the quality and quantity of habitats, and thus determines where animals can live.

Mammals

In just a few thousand years, the Thousand Islands have changed from Arctic environment and northern forest to the rich deciduous/evergreen woodland of today. Throughout that time, the mammal life of the region has also changed remarkably.

When a warming climate melted the glaciers of the last ice age, Arctic wildlife roamed north into the new land. Caribou, Arctic hare, Arctic fox, and wolf lived here—and possibly also the mastodon and the giant beaver and moose, now long extinct. We know that the beluga whale swam in the Champlain Sea, for its skeleton has been found not far from Brockville. By the time that European explorers arrived, animal species and natural communities were well developed. The rich abundance of wildlife overwhelmed the newcomers.

To understand the wildlife patterns of today's Thousand Islands, human beings must be painted into the ecological picture. Humans are, after all, the species of mammal most capable of adapting to or modifying new environments for their needs, and they are perhaps the world's most capable predators. Although the first human records here date from as long ago as 9000 years, the last three centuries have seen the greatest human-generated changes in the environment of the Thousand Islands.

Animals we now equate with wilderness—cougar, lynx, moose, marten, fisher, wolverine, black bear and timber wolf—were a part of this forest scene when French explorers arrived in the seventeenth century. During settlement, trapping and hunting reduced some wildlife populations, but the most extensive and permanent change came from the clearing and developing of the land. As the animals' habitat was taken over, they lost their shelter, refuge and food supply. Large tracts of natural land are required by certain mammals for territories and for maintaining an adequate population size. Many of the original wildlife species could no longer survive here. One mammal, an eastern subspecies of elk, became extinct by 1850.

On the other hand, some of the mammals we now know in the Thousand Islands came here because of human changes to the environment, and others became more numerous in the modified habitats. Cottontail rabbits, for example, first moved north into Canada in the late 1800s, reaching this region about 1925. Coyotes entered Ontario in the early 1900s by way of a route north of the Great Lakes; the open land and lack of timber wolves, which prey on coyotes, was to their liking. Meadow voles, red fox, skunk, woodchuck and white-tailed deer have adapted well to the mix of farmland and woodlot environments and have increased in population. Two other mammals not only live on our doorstep but also have moved right indoors. We have been good to the house mouse and Norway rat by providing them with free rides from Europe and by preparing the type of environment in which they thrive.

There is another group of mammals of interest in the Thousand Islands: those that occasionally invade the area from southern regions. The opossum and gray fox fall into this category. Since 1850, there have been four periods in which the opossum has come into southern Ontario here, most recently in 1961 and 1982. Not actually suited to this climate, northward-venturing opossum usually have ears and tails made stubby by frostbite. The gray fox returned to this area in 1942 after a 300-year absence. A shy, rare animal of forest and marsh, the gray fox is seldom seen.

Could the forests of the Thousand Islands ever again see all of the wildlife of days gone by? Probably not, for there will never again be sufficient woodland to sustain it. Every few years, a wandering black bear, moose or fisher provides an exciting sighting, but these are no doubt isolated cases. Nonetheless, observant residents and visitors in the region are treated to frequent views of small mammals. Porcupines, red foxes, flying squirrels, gray squirrels, mink, long-tailed weasels, ermine, white-tailed deer and many rodents and bats are common in forest, marsh and field. Although the big and far-ranging animals are perhaps gone forever, the wildlife that remains still displays the rich diversity of these natural communities.

Porcupines are good climbers

White-footed mouse

White-tailed deer

Common tern in flight

Kestrel dining on a shrew

Birds

If any bird should be identified with the Thousand Islands, it is that gangling, intensely patient humorist and acrobat, the great blue heron. Spend a little time among the islands and you too will have a heron tale to tell. Just at last light, watch one swoop round a point on grey-blue wings in the blue-grey gloom. If you are near its intended twilight perch, you will be roundly rebuked in heronese that translates into indignation, scorn and honest profanity. Find a great blue at marsh edge, poised with tunnel vision concentration for a thrust at a pumpkinseed sunfish. If it connects, you will see its body language spell out pride, but if it misses, you will observe an unmistakable who-cares sulk. A few springs ago, one well-travelled heron returned to the islands, prepared to show off its latest learned trick: how to float like a duck. Perhaps sensing that this was not routine heron behaviour, the bird flew up and down a stretch of river, landing in deep water obviously just for fun and "kwarking" and grunting with pleasure. Soon, all the great blue herons in that stretch of river were landing like ungainly ducks. And you won't want to miss the heron that straddles the automobile tire mooring buoy near Poole's Resort Island, rocking it back and forth . . . The cast of characters goes on and on.

Interestingly enough, in comparison with the great blue heron, most of the birds in the Thousand Islands are rather inconspicuous. Even in spring, when the numbers of bright and boisterous birds are near their peak, the region may seem quiet to the casual observer. This is because there is no landform to funnel the birds through a small area, though there are numerous migrators. True, the islands are convenient stepping-stones around the east end of Lake Ontario, but the stepping-stones fall in an 80-km-long stretch of river. To run up a good list in the Thousand Islands, you must be a truly dedicated birder.

Still mornings in late March or early April are a good time for birders to visit the river shore between Mallorytown Landing

Great blue heron

of the national park and Brown's Bay. Spring break-up opens a channel that has long been a major gathering place for northbound waterfowl. With good timing, you may find 10,000 ducks in the area, and single large rafts of greater scaup can number 3000 birds. As many as twenty-one species of waterfowl, including snow geese, Canada geese and brant, have been seen in a day. Binoculars and spotting scopes are well worthwhile to note behaviour and courtship displays.

In birdwatching circles, the Thousand Islands is known as the place to see the wild turkey in Canada. These birds are no doubt descendents of turkeys brought to the area in the 1930s, '50s and '60s. Originally they inhabited oak-chestnut woodlands of the northeastern United States and southern Ontario, but were extirpated in most of the northern part of their range when the mature forests were cut. Although it is not totally clear whether a population of turkeys did once naturally inhabit this area, today's small groups do well in summer in the old oak-pine woods and make forays to feeders in the harshest winters.

Although gulls and terns seem a part of the everyday river scene, their populations are undergoing dramatic changes. These changes literally started with a bang late in the last century. When a bizarre fad saw ring-billed gull plumage sought after as adornment on ladies' hats, ring-bills were virtually eliminated. In the decades that followed, the ever-opportunistic herring gull moved inland from its usual coastal habitat to fill the void. By the early 1970s, ring-bills began making a comeback. Although they also suffered setbacks in those same years as a result of agricultural pesticide use, DDT in particular, public awareness led to the use of wiser alternatives, and ring-billed gulls now appear to have regained their ground. In fact, today's populations have exceeded those of old. There are presently fewer than ten gull and tern nesting islets in the Thousand Islands and the ring-bill dominates nearly all of these, with only two or three herring gull nests to be found on some islets. The common tern too may soon be crowded out.

Years from now, white-winged birds will still wheel in these skies, but which species will top the final population balance in the territorial struggle is not yet known. A disturbance as simple as a visit to a colony during the nesting and fledgling season can bring failure to an otherwise successful colony. Birdwatchers are advised to stay clear of the islets where nesting occurs, particularly in June and July.

Fish

For more than a century, fishing for largemouth and smallmouth bass, northern pike and muskellunge has lured sportsmen to the Thousand Islands from all over eastern North America, and sportsfishing there has financed many a fine lodge and guideboat.

Beneath the blue-green surface of the St. Lawrence River lies a landscape as varied as that above water—steep-walled troughs, broken rock, shoals, mud, sandy flats and swift-water narrows. It is estimated that eighty-eight different species of fish live in these waters. With so many different underwater habitats, there is a great variety of small fish, which we popularly lump together as minnows, serving as prey for the large numbers of game fish.

A good place to view fish is from a rock overhanging a rocky shelf or bay in about a metre of water. Smallmouth bass spawn in such areas in mid-June. With rapid sweeps of their tails, they clear silt from a likely patch of stones to create a nest. The male aggressively guards the site and waits for a female to come along. In the wings are rock bass, pumpkinseed sunfish and perch. If the male bass should stray from the nest, the other fish are quick to dash in and eat the eggs. It is therefore vital for the male smallmouth bass to react fast so that the eggs will hatch unharmed. Anything that passes through the bass' territory will be attacked. Unfortunately for the fish, this includes fishing lures, which are seen as just another invader, and so many a nest is left to be plundered early in the fishing season.

Fishing near Thousand Islands Parkway

Later in the summer, schools of bluntnose minnows, spot-tail shiners, rock bass, perch and pumpkinseed sunfish hover in the cool shade under moored boats, swimming with the boat as it drifts back and forth on its lines. Fish are much less wary when approached underwater. To meet the fish face to face, don mask, snorkel and fins and paddle quietly about in a protected bay. You will have a good chance to observe their behaviour in their own habitat and may even see such primitive southern fish as the bowfin or long-nosed gar.

Reptiles and Amphibians
Anyone wishing to become acquainted with one of the world's most myth-burdened group of animals, the reptiles and amphibians, will

find the Thousand Islands an appropriate place. The region is one of the richest in Canada in terms of numbers of species. This animal group reflects well the "tension zone" ecology, where many populations are near their range limits, particularly in Ontario.

One unforgettable creature is the black rat snake, Canada's largest, which can reach lengths to 2.5 m but averages about half

Midland painted turtle   *Black rat snake*

39

Black rat snake

that. Shiny black with faint gold patterning, it would seem hard to overlook, but few people are fortunate enough to see it because of where it hunts and dens. It is an excellent climber and hunts far above the ground in the limits of trees, preying on small birds and eggs. A search for mice may also take the snake to barns, sheds, orchards and fields. It explores and takes refuge among broken rock and in hollow trees and crawls under loose leaves of the forest floor. Black rat snakes have a fondness for sunbasking in spring, which unfortunately lures them onto sun-warmed asphalt where they are all too often run over.

In spite of its large size and often intimidating behaviour—it uses its rattleless tail to thrash the grass or leaves as a warning of its presence—this snake is harmless, and is not poisonous. Loss of suitable habitat has reduced its original range to a fragment of its former size. The Thousand Islands–Rideau Lakes region is one of the last places where it is found in any numbers in Canada.

The garter snake is the most numerous of the species of snakes found in the park and area. It frequents several habitats, such as open woodlands, fields, marsh edges, thickets and shores, to feed on insects, earthworms, frogs, toads and other small creatures. Very similar at a glance is the eastern ribbon snake. Like the garter snake, it has yellow stripes on its flanks, but its tail is longer and much more slender. The known eastern range limit in Ontario for the ribbon snake is at Jones Creek, just east of Mallorytown Landing.

Rocky shores are the home of the northern water snake. This dark, thick, muscular reptile enjoys sunbathing on rocks or logs near the water's edge but scrambles for the water the moment it senses danger. Water snakes, as their name suggests, are excellent swimmers and divers. They feed on frogs and small fish, especially those fish that have recently died.

Frogs are more often seen than heard. The baritone "jug-o-rum" of bullfrogs and the shrill trill of American toads fill the early summer evening air at the marsh edge. Late April to early May is a fine time for a twilight visit to a swamp or swale. Chorus frogs, spring peepers, green frogs, gray tree frogs and leopard frogs announce their presence to the female frogs and with their distinctive voices define their territories to other males. Take along a flashlight and walk softly.

There are few very large populations of reptiles or amphibians in the Thousand Islands because the rugged landscape does not lend itself to extensive areas of suitable habitats. As well, no single area has all of the recorded species, though Hill Island has all nine species of the snakes and many of the frogs found in the region. The Landon's Bay area is also quite rich. In any case, the list of reptiles and amphibians present here is not likely complete. Discoveries of these secretive animals are no doubt yet to be made.

GARDEN OF THE GREAT SPIRIT

W inds rattle leaves loose from the trees, and they end their silent glides on the earth below. Rain and frost and thaw weather pebbles to sand, and sand to dust. Soil becomes richer with the decay of the life it supports and from minerals released from the rock. Rain is an ally of gravity, washing soil to pockets of low ground or into the river.

Soil formation is a process of give and take. Some shores are destined to be bare rock; others accumulate sand and soil, which becomes steadily deeper and richer through the centuries. The island campsite erodes at the water's edge but gathers soil farther back from the shore, gaining overall. A traveller's losses or refuse at the campsites are claimed by the soil. The passage of time sees a growing record—a traveller's account—accumulate in the layers of the campsite floor.

THE CAMPSITE

It is nearly dark on the island now. The last blue and magenta glow of evening fades from sky and water. Details of the landscape have vanished; only silhouettes remain. Pines murmur, wavelets slap, a song sparrow trills a last note, and night spirits settle in the campsite to share tales of other nights, other times.

The campsite has been host to humans since the forest was young. It has been a place to hunt and fish, to rest a night in a long journey, to wait out a storm, and to simply relax. There is good shelter here, a

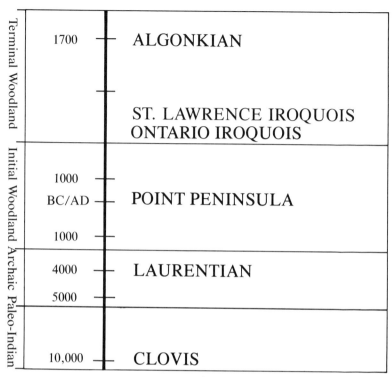

Terminal Woodland	1700 —|—	ALGONKIAN
		ST. LAWRENCE IROQUOIS ONTARIO IROQUOIS
Initial Woodland	1000 BC/AD —|— 1000 —|—	POINT PENINSULA
Archaic	4000 —|— 5000 —|—	LAURENTIAN
Paleo-Indian	10,000 —|—	CLOVIS

Time chart

cool, mosquito-chasing breeze, and the ground dries quickly after a rain. A viewpoint scans the river, and fishing in the nearby shallows is excellent. This campsite is on Gordon Island, and it has a particular story to tell. But there is no doubt that this island's campfire tale is just one of many to be told in the Garden of the Great Spirit.

Nomadic hunters and explorers by nature, the first people came to the Thousand Islands perhaps about 7000 B.C. Very little is known of their material possessions; nothing is known of their lifestyle and language. The people and their era are called "Plano Culture." We do know they hunted large animals. In groups, they brought down even mammoths and mastodons, the woolly elephants that became extinct shortly after the last ice age. Their usual prey, though, was likely woodland caribou, elk and moose—animals that lived in woodlands resembling today's northern forests.

A fragment of a stone hunting point, typically the work of Plano

Culture people, was found at the Gordon Island campsite. We can only speculate about why they were there and probably at other islands. Their prey may have been easier to outwit in a confined area. The fishing in nearby shallows would have been good. Perhaps a family or band chose the island for security from rivals or from a marauding bear. Did they wade over gravel bar shallows, or did they use a dugout canoe? Did they cross the ice in winter? The only hard fact that remains is the fragment of flint.

As populations increased throughout eastern North America, new ideas and technologies developed. In the Archaic period from 5000 B.C. to 1000 B.C., a culture called "Laurentian" evolved in what is now southern Ontario, neighbouring New York and Quebec. While still a hunting society, the people improved their ability to work in the materials at hand: wood, bone, hides and stone. Extensive trade networks came about involving hand-to-hand bartering rather than long distance travel. Trade brought in new materials such as copper from the western Lake Superior area, shells from the southern Atlantic seaboard and Gulf of Mexico, and flint and slate from the future Pennsylvania.

The people were limited in their food resources by what was to be found in the wilderness around them. Like their ancestors of the Plano Culture, the Laurentian people relied on large animals for their main food supply. Even so, it was practical to take advantage of local and seasonal resources such as nuts and berries, bird roosts and spawning fish. It was probably an awareness that fishing and waterfowl hunting would be good in the nearby shallows which brought these people to the campsite as early as 4000 B.C.

Summer months lingered longer at the campsite those many thousands of years ago than at present. The warming trend that ended the last ice age continued until average yearly temperatures were perhaps 5°C warmer than today. More southerly plants and animals could live here because of the long growing season and milder winter. It was probably at that time that the nut-bearing trees such as hickory, hazel, beech and oak came to the forest of the Thousand Islands. Late summer at the campsite would see not only fall flocks of waterfowl in nearby reed beds but a bounty from the trees and bushes as well.

From 500 B.C. to A.D. 500 was a particularly busy time at the site. Good hunting and fishing continued to draw native peoples to the island to enjoy the golden autumn before moving off to winter hunting grounds. The same fire rings were used many times, and the ground around them was tramped hard and bare.

Pottery, baked from sandy clay, developed farther to the south and was adopted by the Archaic people, as they were then called, about

Indians on the St. Lawrence River

Campfire hearth, Gordon Island dig

1500 B.C. The pots were fragile containers and could not stand being set over flames, but they were waterproof and good for storing foods. Fire-hot stones dropped inside them would bring the contents to a boil. Fire-cracked stones began to litter the hearth and campsite.

At perhaps the tenth century A.D., corn agriculture was introduced to the people of this area. Sometimes, the potential of even major new ideas is slow to be understood. It was years before the effect of agriculture was felt. But eventually the people came to rely on corn, and later on beans and squash as well, to offset the uncertainty of the hunt. No longer was there a need to roam so far for food, and the lack of food as a population control diminished. There was more time for creative thought, exchange of ideas . . . and war. Distinct refinements in this the Point Peninsula culture eventually led to another recognizable culture: the Ontario Iroquois.

At the Iroquois campsite, familiar patterns of late-summer island life continued. Perhaps corn was basic to the meals, but deer, bear, beaver, hare, muskrat, raccoon, turtle, catfish and clams all found their way into the cooking pot. Young girls worked with their mothers learning to make pottery and so came to repeat the traditional shapes and patterns. Boys, not unlike country boys today, hunted and fished, swam in the shallows, and wrestled over points of honour, or just for fun. From their fathers they learned how to stalk animals in the forest, how to work in wood and stone, and no doubt they absorbed paternal thoughts on politics and the conduct of the hunt. Inevitably, some object would break or be lost and get scuffed into the earth as another memento of the campsite.

After the thirteenth or fourteenth century A.D., use of the campsite began to decline. Did the islands now lie near a border or frontier? Were different factions forming and defending territories? Archaeological finds in the upper St. Lawrence River area, dating in the centuries not long before the first European explorers arrived, suggest that the Thousand Islands may have been a frontier area between two nations. The Ontario Iroquois, the foundation of the Neutral, Erie, Huron and Petun tribes, appears to have ventured into at least the western section of the Thousand Islands. The League Iroquois—the Onondaga, Mohawk, Oneida, Seneca and Cayuga people—dwelled in parts of the St. Lawrence valley to the south of Lake Ontario. A third group, the St. Lawrence Iroquois, lived in the Lake St. Francis area and north of the St. Lawrence River.

A fourth group, the Algonkians, lived on the Canadian Shield, of which the Frontenac Arch is a southern extension. Their pottery and rock paintings have been found in the Thousand Islands and in adjacent New York state. The Algonkians were loosely allied to the Hurons, but like them, were enemies of the New York Iroquois. Perhaps the occasional foray of the Algonkians into this region kept these other two groups apart. A single piece of an Algonkian pot and one piece of a St. Lawrence Iroquois vessel have been found at the campsite.

Gordon Island lies a little apart from the other islands, but not far from the mainland shore. Through the early historic period, the campsite hosted many who travelled the river highway by canoe and bateau. A worn French gunflint, possibly from the 1600s, was lost or discarded there. A King George III penny, dated 1775, and a broken clay pipe from the same period were added to the campsite's growing collection. A variety of other materials, not glamorous to be sure, enrich the site: battered hand-forged nails, bits of bent and punctured sheet iron, part of a clasp knife, a tiny pile of lead shot of mixed sizes, pieces of glass, and lumps of coal. On the surface of the site lay recent things such as bottle caps and plastic, seemingly as worthless today as the broken pots must have been a thousand years ago.

To the traveller today: listen to the night in your campsite; walk the breeze-cool shores, and rest for a moment on a convenient rock where your view overlooks the channels and isles. Others have paused there, perhaps this year or thousands of years ago. Your heart will tell you that all have enjoyed the scene. Treat the islands as the special places they are, for the night spirits will recall you in their story a thousand years from now.

BY BARK CANOE

The muted thud of paddle on gunnel marked weary, rhythmic time for those in laden bark canoes. The adventure and romance of upriver travel by canoe soon became the muscle-straining, leg-cramping work of conquering current, rapids and head wind. Explorers, traders, missionaries, military men and adventurers from Europe, especially from France, made that journey from Montreal to destinations on Lake Ontario and beyond. The St. Lawrence River tested the mettle of the travellers, and became a well-known passage. The rugged granite Thousand Islands, so different from anything else experienced by river travellers, were not a destination but a gateway to frontiers and a milestone on the route to the heart and challenge of a new land.

Explorer Jacques Cartier, on his second voyage of discovery to Canada, did not endear himself, or the French in general, to the Iroquois; he kidnapped several persons including a prominent chief. For some years thereafter, travel to the upper St. Lawrence River, commonly known then as the River of the Iroquois, was an unwise risk of life and limb. The preferred inland route until the mid-1650s was the Ottawa River.

Samuel de Champlain, an insatiable adventurer, was perhaps the first European to glimpse the Thousand Islands. Accompanying Huron warriors on an expedition against the Onondaga of Upper New York in 1615, Champlain crossed Lake Ontario at its eastern end. After an unsuccessful military encounter, he returned across the lake. Skirting the west edge of Wolfe and Simcoe islands, and crossing from there to the mainland, he noted the presence of more islands a little to the east but was probably not in the mood to describe much else. He had been wounded in a leg and knee and was being packed off contrary to his desires to a Huron encampment to recover.

In 1653, Jesuit Father Simon Le Moyne made peace between the French and the Onondagas. Perhaps the peace was too little too late for what the French might have accomplished in North America, but the respite at least allowed the French access to the upper St. Lawrence River. On 17 July 1654, Le Moyne left Montreal during another journey into Iroquois country. Ten hard days of travel brought him to the Thousand Islands. He wrote: "The 27th. We coast along the shores of the lake, everywhere confronted by towering rocks, now apalling, now pleasing to the eye. It is wonderful how large trees can find root among so many rocks." The lake Le Moyne mentions is the first of many references to the "Lac des Milles-Isles," or Lake of the Thousand Islands.

A route commonly followed through the islands took early canoeists past the site of present-day Brockville, along the river's north shore, between Grenadier and Tar islands, and between Hill and Wellesley islands through Lake of the Isles. The narrow course above Lake of the Isles was called "Petite Detroit," or little straits, known today as the International Rift. A brief ceremony and celebration was held at the end of this passage, for when canoeists reached this point, they knew the hardships of upriver travel were over and another phase of the journey would begin. Although this route was too shallow for the larger boats of later years to use, it allowed the canoeists to avoid most of the strong currents of the main channels.

The French were ever mindful of the presence of the Iroquois people of eastern Ontario and upper New York. Locations and names of Iroquois villages were recorded and mapped during their travels. Beginning in 1656, a village called Toniata was noted near the east end of the Thousand Islands, generally in the Grenadier Island–Jones Creek area. The people were probably Onondaga, the group with whom Le Moyne had made peace. Curiously, there is no record that any explorer or missionary ever visited the village even though it appeared in records again and again for nearly 125 years.

The Iroquois people were by this time an alliance of five nations. All found their traditional territories and way of life being radically changed. England, France, the Netherlands and to a lesser degree Sweden, sought control over sections of resource-rich east-central North America. Europeans often seemed ruthless in their attitudes towards the resources and the peoples of the land. Resistance or co-existence were not always clear-cut options for the Iroquois. Decreased populations of wildlife, new diseases, pressure on their territories from neighbouring peoples, and the lure of wealth from trade in furs were new and sometimes cruel influences on the traditional way of life.

Through the years, intrepid explorer-missionaries travelled through the Thousand Islands to face hazards and perhaps hostilities in the interior of North America. The names of many are widely known because of their contributions to our knowledge of the land and the people: Pierre Esprit Radisson, Médard Chouart des Groseilliers, François Dollier de Casson and René Bréhant de Galinée are but a few of these brave men. Another who passed this way was Louis de Buade, best known as Count Frontenac, then governor of New France. Decisions made by Frontenac were of great importance to the future of the upper St. Lawrence River and eastern Lake Ontario.

By the late 1660s, it was clear that the peace with the Iroquois was really little more than a truce. Even the relatively limited North

American empire envisioned by King Louis XIV of France could be lost if there were no means to control the Iroquois and to ensure the continued traffic of furs to Montreal.

Late in the spring of 1671, Governor Rémy de Courcelles mounted an unprecedented project. His goal was to take a strong military force to Lake Ontario as rapidly as possible in order to impress the Iroquois, and to note a potential location for a fort. The trip upriver took only ten days and the return took five. His flotilla of thirteen canoes included a heavy bateau, the first to be taken up the St. Lawrence. This achievement was to open the way for future commercial traffic.

Count Frontenac replaced Courcelles as governor the following year, and he too realized the importance of a firm French presence in Lake Ontario. Frontenac assembled at Montreal a flotilla of 120 canoes, 2 bateaux and about 400 men in late June 1673. His original destination was Quinte where Iroquois of both shores of Lake Ontario were gathered to meet him in conference, and where he had thought to build a fort.

Before he arrived at Quinte, messengers met Frontenac to inform him that a gathering there could be interpreted as a sign of preference of the Quinte Indians over those of the south shore. Frontenac made a crucial decision, and avoided an error in diplomacy. He went instead to the mouth of the Cataraqui River where he chanced to find an ideal site for his purposes.

By the end of July, a wooden fort at Cataraqui was completed. The French at last had a frontier post. It would become a check against the Indians and English, a mission, a trading post, and a supply link to other posts on Lake Ontario. It became known as Fort Frontenac, after its founder, and was the future site of the city of Kingston. In the next two decades, the worth and future of the fort were much debated by the French. Fort Frontenac was abandoned for a short time after 1689 when it seemed that it could not be held against the Indians, who were supported by the English.

An uneasy peace between the English and French came to a dramatic close when both sides armed themselves anew in their long-standing rivalries over the land and its rich resources. In the spring of 1756, the French General Montcalm attacked and captured Fort Bull and Fort Ontario on the Oswego River. The attack had originated at Fort Frontenac and no doubt served to show the English the strategic significance of the French fort which could dominate eastern Lake Ontario while being supplied up the St. Lawrence River.

Lt. Col. John Bradstreet assembled a British force in 1758 at Fort Ontario, the very fort the French had taken only two years before.

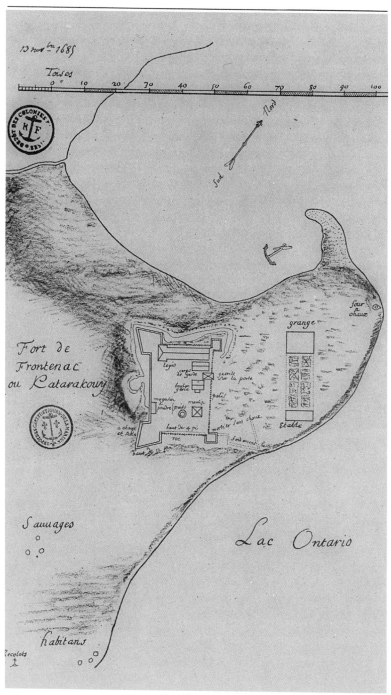

Fort Frontenac

The capture of Fort Frontenac

Bradstreet's objective was to defeat the French at Fort Frontenac as part of a major British assault on French strongholds in Canada. Fort Frontenac had been built when the only menace was poorly armed Indians. The 110-man garrison of the antiquated fort could not withstand the British assault of 3600 men and a pounding from eight cannons. It fell to the British at 8:00 A.M., 26 July 1758. This victory became the first in a series of successes along the St. Lawrence that eventually delivered French Canada to the British in 1763.

The French were the first to explore and map the Thousand Islands, but there are few tangible signs that they once held title to this land. When the English fought their way to control, the area remained unsettled for another generation. However, for the first time in a century and a half, travellers through the region did not have to fear ambush at every hidden passage in the isles.

THE LOST CHANNEL

On 14 August 1760, the greatest military force ever to sail the upper St. Lawrence River set out from Grenadier Island, near Cape Vincent. Gen. Jeffrey Lord Amherst commanded the 10,124 men, 2 ships—the *Onondaga* and the *Mohawk*—72 whale-boats, 177 bateaux, and various supply boats. The British expedition was on its way to attack the French Fort de Lévis, east of present-day Prescott. Then they planned to continue downriver to capture Montreal.

As Amherst's fleet rounded into the south channel of the river, a masthead lookout saw a French bateau pull into the stream. Its crew obviously intended to warn the force at Fort de Lévis. Captain Loring of the *Onondaga* set out in pursuit, but the French bateau easily stayed ahead of the larger vessel. The chase led past Wellesley Island and into the channel at Wallace and Lyndoch islands where the bateau suddenly vanished.

As darkness set in, Loring realized they had been ambushed. The *Onondaga* was swept with musket fire, and arrows whistled shrilly into the decks. At the same moment, the swift current seemed about to hurl the ship into a cliff face. While the *Onondaga*'s crew drove the French and Indians back with cannon and musket, a boat was lowered to warn the *Mohawk*. A second boat, lowered to find an escape route, succeeded in leading the *Onondaga* clear of the treacherous channel. When the ship was safely at anchor, a crew under Ensign Barry was sent back to find the first boat. Unable to locate either the boat or the channel, he named the place "The River of the Lost Channel."

Two or three years later, the crew of a passing bateau found a smashed and sunken yawl bearing the name *Onondaga* at the head of the swift channel between Constance and Georgina islands.

The Lost Channel

Pine power (near Rockport)

SETTLEMENT

Amid the Thousand Islands, one may feel either intimacy or intimidation in the abrupt appearance of lichen-grey granite and winding channels. From the seemingly impenetrable rocks rise lofty white pines, slow-tapered and flagged away from the wind: centuries-old sentinels guarding yet guiding the way through the maze of islands.

To the Indians, the Thousand Islands were the Garden of the Great Spirit, a bountiful summer and fall encampment. To the French, the islands signalled the final day's journey to Lake Ontario, but though impressive for their scenery, were considered of value only for their natural resources. For a long time, the Thousand Islands remained a sparsely populated wilderness on a waterway to the interior of the continent. Then, with the close of the British-French conflict in North America in 1763, came the circumstances that would bring settlement to the region.

The Loyalists

The wars between the French and British had been enormously expensive. Britain sought to reduce its debt by taxing the Thirteen Colonies on the Atlantic Coast to recover at least part of the costs. After all, the economy of the colonies had benefitted greatly when trade routes were opened and protected during the British conquest of North America.

The American colonists had paid duties on imports but had otherwise been left to run most of their own affairs. Taxes were viewed as interference in their business. Eventually, there came a boycott of British goods, open rebellion, and then hostile division between those loyal to Britain and those united by common cause against her. By the late 1760s, particularly at Boston, British officials as well as merchants who traded in British goods were provoked in the streets and in the press. They began to leave, some for England, and others to Canada—then known as Quebec—to share in its development.

56

Through the 1770s, the situation grew rapidly worse, erupting in the War of American Independence. Those loyal to Britain had the choice of disavowing their loyalty: to fight or to flee. In the heat of revolution, British troops were often joined by the Loyalists, and Loyalist militia units were formed. All who took up arms or fled abandoned their property and much of their personal wealth. When peace was signed at the Treaty of Paris, 3 September 1783, Britain faced the issue of settling Loyalists in Canada. Many settled in Quebec or in the Maritimes, but the largest numbers were systematically settled in as yet unpopulated areas of Ontario.

River Settlements

Two sets of townships were rapidly surveyed west of Montreal. The first set, known as the Royal Townships, lay east of the Thousand Islands. A second set, the Cataraqui Townships, were laid out to the west of the Thousand Islands along the Bay of Quinte area. Where the ragged Frontenac Arch cut through the lowlands, the land was considered much less valuable because it was difficult to farm. Consequently, the survey of the island region was left until last. The Royal Townships were largely allocated to Sir John Johnson's and Major Jessup's corps, both of whom had been active in campaigns in New York state. Settled there too were groups of disbanded soldiers and their families from many regiments, and a group known as "unincorporated" Loyalists—those who had come independently to Canada as refugees.

Early in 1784, the resettlement began with a difficult journey upriver by bateaux. The settlers could do little clearing and building that first summer. Surveys, the selection of lots, and the move to the land took up a good deal of time, even though the massive undertaking of the settlement program was remarkably well organized. Once they arrived in the township that was chosen for them, the settlers drew numbered cards from a hat to ensure luck-of-the-draw in their selection of properties. Officers drew first for lots along the concessions closest to the river.

Although the westernmost of the nine Royal Townships was Elizabethtown, in which Brockville is now located, some Loyalists were settled that first year in two other townships: Front of Yonge and Front of Escott. The surveys of Front of Leeds and Lansdowne and Front of Escott were done in 1788; Pittsburgh Township in 1789, and the Front of Yonge in 1794. The islands were included in the various townships fronting on the river but were not included in the first draw for lots and grants.

Quite naturally, the first land in all of the townships to be settled was within a few concessions of the river, since the St. Lawrence was the only major transportation route. Those settlers who were granted land near the back of the townships, or who were discouraged by the quality of land they received, traded, bartered or sold their lots. As well, many who received grants in the first years did not immediately settle. The Thousand Islands remained sparsely populated for some time.

Although many of the oldest communities along the St. Lawrence are those nearest the river, ridges and cliffs line the river between Brockville and Gananoque. As a result, villages developed along the second concession, about one and a half kilometres inland. Even so, for other than local transportation, the river was all-important. Each inland village had a roadway link to the river front where a dock could be built. Mallorytown Landing, Rockport and Ivy Lea (Lansdowne Dock) were ports for Mallorytown, Escott and Waterton, and Lansdowne respectively.

Onto the Land

Adiel Sherwood, son of Elizabethtown Township's first settler, and who became sheriff of Johnstown, wrote the following observation about the land to which the Loyalists came: "At that time, the country was a howling wilderness. Not a tree had been cut by an actual settler, from the Province Line to Kingston, a distance of 150 miles."

With no road, no track, no house in view, there was no sign that any man had ever set foot on the land. Even on sunny summer days the hemlock-lined ravines were dark and damp and cool as night. Mammoth white oaks of imponderable age brooded over sedge and boulder-strewn hillsides. In broad valleys beneath the sweeping limbs of hickory, beech and maple, all was still. Gnarled pitch pine weathered on the sunswept windward rocks. In the shelter of the pitch pine and red oak, white pine rose and touched the sky. Settlers exploring the ridge tops marvelled at the granite so finely split and wedged apart by the living force of the giant white pine's roots.

How formidable the task of clearing the land must have been! The tools were axe and hoe and little else in the first years. For many, even simple household tools and furnishings were luxuries. A majority of the Loyalists had been tradesmen, merchants, carpenters and farmers. There were probably no better people to settle the land, for these Loyalists had courage, ingenuity and a sense of purpose. They were pioneers in the truest sense.

A first settlement

Log shanties, perhaps 5 x 6 m in size with one door and one window, gave rustic shelter at the beginning. Furniture was rough and hand-made. Clearing the land to plant the first crops of wheat, corn, squash and potatoes—all but the wheat was native to the Americas—was a priority. Shortages of seed, implements, farm animals and food itself caused a terrible hardship here as elsewhere, especially in the Hungry Years of 1788–89. The settlers had to look to the woods for their meat and for wild plants to provide variety in, if not the total substance of, their diet.

Fortunately, wild animals were still abundant. Moose, elk, deer, bear, snowshoe hare, passenger pigeon, grouse and waterfowl were the basis of many a meal. Furs of marten, fisher, lynx and timber wolf added warmth to winter clothing and provided extra income when they could be sold.

But by the late 1700s, hunting and settlement brought about great changes in the wildlife populations and their habitats. Many of the animals mentioned above were lost to the region. It is quite probable that most of the overhunting was unintentional. There were mouths to feed, and the wilderness seemed endless. On the other hand, some settlers apparently hunted for pleasure: one man's excessive harvest was 192 deer, 34 bears and 46 wolves on his farm alone.

The Community of the Thousand Islands

By the close of the eighteenth century, surpluses of grain began the steady trend towards prosperity in the district. Huts and log shanties were abandoned for frame, stone or brick houses. Substantial barns and sheds replaced lean-tos. Specialty outbuildings such as smokehouses, icehouses, woodsheds and sugar shacks became part of the growing farm complexes. But the lack of large mills, especially flour mills, was both inconvenient for the settlers and a limitation to the economy.

The government financed and controlled the operation of the early mills. The first, Kingston Mill, was built in 1784 and for many years was the only one for some distance around. Farmers from as far away as Brockville had to take their wheat to Kingston by canoe, bateau or in winter by sled over the frozen river.

The Gananoque River had two very good falls of water near the St. Lawrence River. One of the falls was harnessed in 1792 by Sir John Johnson. Joel Stone, who is credited as being the founder of Gananoque, built a second mill in 1795. When the government eased the restrictions on mills, and as imports and foundries made millstones and iron more readily available, mill sites at Yonge's Mills, Lyn and Brockville were exploited. William La Rue built a gristmill and sawmill on La Rue Creek, just west of Mallorytown Landing, in the early 1800s.

All of these mills were of great importance to the settlers in the Thousand Islands. By the 1830s, the McDonald Mill in Gananoque was producing more flour than any other mill in the province. It had a capacity of 250 barrels a day and accounted for about 25 percent of the flour received at the port of Montreal.

The early settlers also faced a shortage of iron. All types of tools, equipment, pots and machine parts had to be brought from England, from the small forge at Three Rivers (now Les Forges du Saint-Maurice National Historic Park), or sometimes from the United States. Iron goods had a value beyond dollars to the settlers because of poor supply and agonizingly slow transportation. Fortunately for those who lived in this region, Dr. James Schofield came to Canada from Connecticut in 1795 and immediately set about building an iron works—the first in Upper Canada. Although the ore was of poor quality, Schofield's forge at Furnace Falls (now Lyndhurst) was producing a half tonne of cast iron and nearly 200 kg of wrought iron per day in 1801. Even this relatively brittle iron must have been heartily welcomed. But the low quality of the ore finally forced the operation to close, and fire destroyed the structure in 1811.

Mallorytown was a vital little community in the early 1800s. A good deal of the progress in the village was due to the efforts of Nathanial Mallory, a Vermont Loyalist who came to Mallorytown Landing in 1784. After a time, Mallory moved inland to the site of the present village to be closer to better farmland. The Mallory family contributed greatly to the community with a good farm, one of four brickyards in the area, and a lumbering and fuelwood cutting industry. Andrew Mallory's most notable achievement of all, though, was to set up the first glassworks in Canada. In about 1825, he began the operations which lasted some fifteen years. The source of silica for the glass was local sandstone, the Potsdam Formation. Iron impurities gave this glass a beautiful aquamarine colour said to resemble the waters of the St. Lawrence on a brilliant day.

Island Farms

References to specific islands were rare in the accounts of travellers or government officials until the mid-1800s. The islands were not included in the original survey of lots in the townships. In the rush to organize the settlement of the countryside, perhaps first glance failed to observe the good farming prospects on some of them.

However, the farming potential on the islands did not go completely unnoticed. One traveller, Robert Gourlay, wrote in 1822:

> In the river, which is very wide, are some large islands of a very superior quality in point of soil, and from whence large supplies of oak and pine timber for the Quebec and Montreal markets have been had. The temperature of the air on the islands in the St. Lawrence is milder than on the main continent, as the tender vegetables thrive more, and come to fuller maturity. This may be owing to the humidity of the atmosphere, occasioned by the large body of water in which they are enveloped.

Grenadier and Hill islands caught the eye of a few of the Loyalists once they were settled on their own mainland farms. Since the river was the route to many of the mills, and villages were not far inland, island farmers were no more isolated from trade and commerce than were mainlanders. Workboats substituted for wagons, and island settlements became communities in their own right. The remains of one old barge which was used to haul farm supplies and produce, including milk to a creamery at Rockport, today lies in the shallow on the north shore of Grenadier Island.

Through the efforts of the first two generations of Loyalists, the limits of wilderness frontier had been pushed far beyond the region of the Thousand Islands. The most sweeping changes in the landscape had been made, and the accomplishments of the people were considerable. The ironworks, glassworks and mills were milestones.

Old mower, Central Grenadier Island

Grain production, though it depleted the land, had created the agricultural setting that saw Leeds County become the second ranking producer of butter and cheese in Ontario by 1850.

Lumbering too had been an important source of income for the farmers, but the settlers had cleared only where it seemed practical and so the ridge and lowland forests were spared. When a growing demand for lumber turned attention to these rugged stands, the biggest and tallest trees were selected. Twisted and ancient specimens that reflected the hardships of life on granite and swampland were left. The pines were felled from the hillsides where they had for so long dominated the skyline and guided the way on the river. Their offspring, in the shelter of their gnarled ancestors, survived. The young pines have grown well in the century of intervening time, taking their place in the hidden seams among the fractured boulders. These pines are tall enough now that it is not difficult to imagine their reaching the sentinel-like stature the first Loyalists knew.

Pitch pines on a rock cliff

GUNS &
STILL WATERS

The history of the Thousand Islands intertwines the lives and livelihood of people on both the Canadian and American shores. Before the War of Independence between Britain and the United States, the St. Lawrence River was a corridor, not a boundary. During the war, the river became the line that Loyalists could cross to find refuge. More than a half century of unrest between the two countries followed the War of Independence. Even so, people along both banks of the Thousand Islands grew cautiously closer and closer together. Certainly the river is a logical political boundary, but it is as well the common focus and unifying force for residents of both banks.

When the British opened the lands along the north shore of the St. Lawrence to Loyalist settlements, the new American government also took an interest in the region. Even as surveys were being completed in the Royal Townships, others were carried out to create ten townships opposite them on the New York shore. This work was completed in the spring of 1787. Free grants of land in Canada had attracted many Americans who sought a new start, but in the United States, the land was sold. The lots in the Ten Towns were put up for public auction that summer in New York City. Alexander Macomb, who had prospered as a fur trader at Detroit, succeeded in acquiring most of the lots and later sold all but a few of them to other speculators.

Soon afterwards, settlers from New York, Vermont and other states purchased lots. Some of the speculators sponsored the construction of the essential mills and towns, and in many ways performed the role that the Canadian government was performing on its side of the river. Indeed, some Canadians moved to these townships where restrictions on mill developments were less oppressive than those in the British territory.

West of the Ten Towns in the United States, through the Thousand Islands to the shores of Lake Ontario only a few individuals had settled and the land remained virtually a wilderness. A great deal of this land and all the way to Oswego was purchased by Count James Donatien Le Ray de Chaumont. Le Ray's father had helped to finance the American Revolution by sending gunpowder to Boston, clothing an army, and outfitting three of the vessels of John Paul Jones.

Count Le Ray's assistance in the war had been costly, so he sent his son to the United States soon after the war to collect debts owed to him. While there, the younger Le Ray became interested in and later purchased large tracts of land. Three of the towns on the American side of the Thousand Islands—Alexandria Bay, Theresa and Cape Vincent—are named after his children. Interestingly, Joseph Bonaparte, brother of Napoleon, and several military leaders who had served with the French emperor purchased land in the Watertown area from Le Ray after their exodus from France upon Napoleon's defeat and exile.

THE WAR OF 1812–14

By the close of the first decade of the 1800s, the young settlements on both riverbanks in the Thousand Islands were taking form. However, because of British naval blockades, American expansionism, commercial rivalry and arrogant stubborness on both sides, Great Britain and the United States drifted closer and closer to conflict. The border of Canada and the United States became the theatre for an inevitable but largely unwanted war. More than one-third of the American House of Representatives and the Senate voted against war. In New York state, eleven of fourteen representatives voted against the declaration, for this state had more to lose than any other since most of their trade was with Canada. War did not put an end to local trade in the areas; it drove it underground.

War was declared by the United States on 18 June 1812. Actually, the British blockade on the Atlantic coast had brought British, American and French ships into sporadic conflict several years before.

Throughout the war, Britain had little difficulty with its supply route to Lower Canada. Upper Canada was another matter. Inland industry was not sufficiently developed to supply an army's needs. It became evident to the British that the St. Lawrence River was a critical yet fragile lifeline for Upper Canada. There were no alternatives. Roads were stump-strewn trails where, if messengers or wagons were not lost to the hazards of the road, they could be easily taken in ambush. Troops and cargo had to travel to the river, a costly and tiring trip requiring about two weeks from Montreal to Kingston. Moreover, the river was not passable in winter.

The Americans, on the other hand, did not have to rely on the St. Lawrence. They had several overland and river routes that had been developed, ironically, by the British during the early trade years and in later episodes against the French. Surprisingly, both sides were slow to take offensive or defensive actions along the upper St. Lawrence, where a stranglehold so easily could have been put upon Canada. Organized raids could have brought river traffic to a standstill.

The first solution to the British supply-line problem came when the Corps of Voyageurs, former employees of the fur-trading North

West Company, was formed to organize a convoy system. This role was taken over by the British army in the spring of 1813. Bateaux and Durham boats carried the equipment of war and goods of commerce. These stopped at prearranged staging points which included Cornwall, Prescott, Brockville, Chimney Island and Gananoque. In most places, the enemy could be seen at a distance on the river. The Thousand Islands, with its myriad of channels and isles, were ideal for concealing raiding parties. A flotilla of nine gunboats was launched to protect convoys through this most treacherous area.

Because of their slow speed and single cannon, gunboats had not been a great success on the lakes, but in the river their versatility and shallow draft made them quite effective. The nine gunboats were divided into three groups of three, with one group stationed at Kingston and a second at Prescott to escort boats through the Thousand Islands. The third was to cruise the islands, especially from Gananoque to Chimney Island, on the prowl for would-be ambushers.

In the early part of the war of 1812–14, military activity did not disrupt trade in the Thousand Islands nor did it affect the region's

Attack of Fort Oswego, 1814

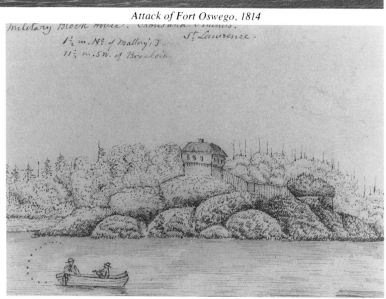

Chimney Island blockhouse, 1813

THE BROWN'S BAY WRECK

The gunboats used for more than half a century by the British Royal Navy to patrol the Baltic Sea, Lake Champlain and the Great Lakes were heavy wooden vessels varying in dimension from 12 to 18 m in length and 2.5 to 5 m of beam. In general, they were wide, shallow-drafted, single-decked vessels without cabins, and had a sloop, schooner, bugger or lateen rig. Since they did not have a keel to prevent sideslip, their best points of sail were away from the wind. However, all were fitted with oars or sweeps so that they could be rowed when sailing was not possible. Gunboats were built with stout oak ribs and pine planks to support the weight and recoil of the single cannon mounted on the broad bow.

Many gunboats were built in British North America, especially at the naval shipyard in Kingston, but none was preserved intact. Following the war, the Rush-Bagot Treaty of 1817 limited the number of armed ships that Britain and the United States could keep in service on inland waters. During the negotiation of the treaty, both sides realized that they could complete fleets and mothball whatever ships they chose; thus a sort of arms race was on.

A century and a half later, National Historic Parks and Sites divers raised the hulk of a gunboat from the sandy shallows of Brown's Bay, just east of Mallorytown Landing. It bore no nameplate, and shifting ice and souvenir hunters had broken away much of the upper structure. Yet with the help of records kept by the Royal Navy, the probable identity of the boat was traced.

The gunboat hulk, now on display at Mallorytown Landing, is quite likely that of the H.M.S. *Radcliffe,* completed 31 March 1817. It was the last boat listed on the Kingston navy yard inventory before the signing of the Rush-Bagot Treaty. For many years, it was kept in good condition: its hull was replanked, and the newer planks were tarred with pine pitch to prevent rot. The first layer of planks had been fastened with copper nails, but by the 1820s, builders knew that iron nails would last the life of a hull in fresh water. Eventually the day came when the steam engine made sail-powered gunboats obsolete. The naval yard received orders to sell what boats it could and to destroy the rest. Interestingly, the *Radcliffe*'s name does not appear on either list.

Modifications to the hull provide clues which help piece together the later years of the gunboat's story. At some point, much of the deck behind the mast was cut away. Planks were laid over the ribs in the floor and a centreboard trunk was built in beside the original keel timber. The old gunboat was made into a cargo carrier that would sail upwind because of the centreboard, thus obviating the need for a large crew. It probably became a farmer's work boat. Scars and gouges in the floor planks suggest that rock, barrels, cattle and timber were among the freight carried.

tranquillity. Fort Henry at Kingston asserted control of the east end of Lake Ontario and the entrance to the river, but was ever vigilant of the American fort and navy at Sacket's Harbor. Fort Wellington at Prescott was the British deterrent to the Americans on the river in the upper river area.

In the summer of 1813, the first regular American troops in northern New York reached Sacket's Harbor. Led by Capt. Benjamin Forsyth, they were assigned that fall to attack Gananoque in order to capture ammunition and unsettle the nerves of the Canadians. This they proceeded to do. The militia were alarmed when Forsyth's approach was discovered, and they greeted him with a volley of musket fire. Most shots missed; Forsyth charged, and the militia fled. In the process of taking the arms and ammunition they had come for, the Americans set fire to several buildings and ransacked Col. Joel Stone's house. The citizens were outraged.

Realizing that Ogdensburg was in a better position to attack British shipping than was Sacket's Harbor, the American troops moved downriver later in the fall after the Gananoque raid. An exploratory attack from Fort Wellington was repulsed from Ogdensburg, and after that everyone was prepared to settle in for the winter. The militia at Ogdensburg were sent home, leaving Captain Forsyth and the troops alone. A man of action, Forsyth decided to raid Brockville to release American prisoners held in jail. After all, the British had crossed the river quite uninvited to retrieve deserters from *their* army. His raid was a success: all but a convicted murderer were released and several citizens of Brockville were escorted back to Ogdensburg. Private property was not molested, but public stores of munitions were taken. In retaliation, the force at Prescott made an attack on the American town. Meeting with less resistance than they had anticipated, the British took the town. They captured a large number of prisoners, eleven cannons, all military stores and burned two schooners. Sacket's Harbor became the only stronghold in the upper St. Lawrence for the United States.

Forsyth's raid on Gananoque had underlined the weak defences in the towns and control points in the river. Blockhouses were erected at Gananoque in 1813 and at Chimney Island in early 1814. The Chimney Island blockhouse could be reached easily from shore over a sandbar, and the military camp was on the ridge back from the river. Chimney Island is at the entrance to the channel along the north shore, and cannons at that place would have covered shipping in the route between Grenadier Island and the mainland.

In the summer of 1813, the American government granted permission of two private boats, the *Neptune* and the *Fox* of Sacket's

Naval engagement in the Thousand Islands

Harbor to become privateers. Their intent was to waylay British convoys in the Thousand Islands. The first ambush was a success, with the capture of sixty-nine prisoners, a twelve-pound cannon, 270 barrels of pork and other military stores. When this news reached Kingston, three gunboats set out in search of the privateers. They followed the American shore to Goose Bay and were joined by a fourth gunboat. The British inched up Cranberry Creek until the way was blocked by freshly felled trees. It was a classic ambush, but in the fight the British regrouped and withdrew. The Americans too beat a hasty retreat. However, when nearing Sacket's Harbor, they were fired upon by H.M.S. *Earl of Moira,* and sank their own boats to avoid their capture.

To put an end once and for all to American raids in the islands, the British navy undertook a sweep of the upper river. They assumed the Thousand Islands would be trouble-free from then on. This was not quite the case. Nearly a year later, another small American raiding force, armed with guns and swords, hid their three light sailboats at the head of Tar Island, near Rockport. Several large convoys of British boats passed by before Sailing Master Gregory, leader of the American party, found something his size. The gunboat *Black Snake,* under Captain Landon and with twenty men, lazed along under sail. Landon, thinking that the three approaching gigs were British, set out by skiff to greet them. Only after he was on board one of them and taken prisoner did he discover the ruse. Gregory quickly took the *Black Snake* in tow and set out for Clayton. Before he reached the south shore, another British gunboat gave pursuit. The *Black Snake* was scuttled near Deer Island but later salvaged intact and repaired at Kingston. The American's light boats outrowed the heavy gunboat to escape.

For the rest of the war, the stillness of the Thousand Islands was not broken. This peace on the St. Lawrence was reinforced by the defeat of the American army at Crysler's Farm, and at the Chateauguay River in the late fall of 1814. The supply line on the river remained intact. Finally, the peace treaty was signed at Ghent, Belgium, on Christmas Eve, 1814.

The War of 1812–14 was in a sense a catalyst for the development of Canada as a nation. At the outset of the war, the majority of the population of Upper Canada had moved there from the United States. Yet time and time again, citizens and militia rallied to the defence of their communities when they were threatened. Nonetheless, changes in the immigration policy were made encouraging people from Great Britain rather than the United States to come to Canada. Many of these people were settled in the townships inland from the St. Lawrence river. The population of Leeds County on which the Thousand Islands front grew from 5900 in 1812 to 9456 in 1825 and to 16,994 in 1835.

From a military point of view, the war had shown the fragility of the St. Lawrence as a link between Upper and Lower Canada. Consequently, the first hydrographic survey of the river was carried out in 1815 by Captain Owen of the Royal Navy. A canal was completed in the course of the Cataraqui and Rideau rivers in 1832 to create a navigable waterway between Kingston and Ottawa. This would allow water-borne traffic to avoid, if it became necessary, the vulnerable route on the St. Lawrence River. The Ottawa River, from Ottawa to Montreal, completed the loop.

On the American side, the counterpart to the Rideau Canal was the Erie Canal, from Albany to Buffalo, which provided access from the Hudson River to Lake Erie, especially for commercial traffic.

THE PATRIOTS' WAR

Despite the fact that many Canadians never faltered in defence of their land, some Americans simply could not free themselves of the opinion that the people of Canada truly loathed life as a British colony. Freedom, they assumed, was a desire of all Canadians which could not be realized under British rule. Accordingly, when the radical Scotsman William Lyon Mackenzie preached reform in Canada, American citizens were among the sympathetic listeners. Mackenzie's followers turned from argument to arms in Toronto in 1837, but fled in their defeat to Buffalo, New York. In the period since the 1812 war, a large number of New Englanders had moved to upstate New York, bringing anti-British sentiment with them. Mackenzie gained support and funds there, and enlisted a motley crew of unemployed adventurers with whom he proposed to invade Canada.

Mackenzie settled himself on Navy Island in the Niagara River, where he set up a "Provisional Government of the Republic of Upper Canada." Taking a dim view of the republic, a small Canadian force captured and burned the rebels' supply ship *Caroline*. After this chilly reception for his republic in Canada, Mackenzie took his invasion elsewhere. A rabble army of perhaps 2000 collected at Clayton. Since they could not begin their invasion from American soil—the United States had voted for neutrality on this issue—they moved instead to Hickory Island, near Grindstone Island. They intended first to frighten the citizens of Gananoque and then capture Kingston. The assault was never launched because the army dwindled from its original number of 200 to 35 men. Very likely the attack would have failed anyway, for Elizabeth Barnett, an American school teacher working in Gananoque, overheard the plans at Clayton and warned her Canadian friends. The word spread fast. At Kingston, excited preparations were made for a fight that never came.

American neutrality had forced the rebels, or patriots as they called themselves, to go underground. A number of secret societies were formed in the United States to aid the rebel Canadians. One of these societies determined to capture the steamer *Sir Robert Peel,* owned by Brockville citizens and captained by John Armstrong—who, the rebels suspected, had been a British spy at Mackenzie's Navy Island camp. The man selected to take the steamer was William Johnston, the self-styled Admiral of the patriot navy, known locally as Pirate Bill Johnston.

During the War of 1812–14, the British had imprisoned Johnston on charges of spying. When released, he turned to raiding British supply parties and to the activity for which he was first arrested. Thereafter, Pirate Bill became the "Canadian Renegade" and smuggler who sought to avenge himself against British authority. Johnston had helped guide American forces under General Williamson downriver in 1813. He must have felt William Lyon Mackenzie's goal of independence for Canada was made to order to vent his long-standing grudge against the British. It was Johnston who guided Mackenzie to Navy Island, and he was to have helped lead the attacks on Gananoque and Kingston.

The *Sir Robert Peel* was loading fuelwood at McDonald's Wharf on Wellesley Island late on the night of 29 May 1838. Captain Armstrong had been warned of a few suspicious characters in the area that day but paid no heed. No watch was kept and the passengers had retired for the night. Suddenly, Johnston and his band of fewer than twenty men leaped dramatically from hiding, dressed and painted like Indians, and hollering. They stormed aboard the ship, waving guns and swords, and unceremoniously herded the passengers, who were in various stages of nightdress, to shore.

After the ship was looted, its boilers were fired, and the rebels cast off. The *Sir Robert Peel* was to have been the start of Johnston's navy. However, not far from shore, the steamer grounded firmly on a shoal. Unable to remove it, Johnston set it afire, burning the ship to the waterline. As they rowed rapidly into the dark of night, the rabble was heard to yell, "Remember the *Caroline*."

Most Americans saw the burning of the *Sir Robert Peel* as simple revenge for the *Caroline*. Canadians, especially in the Thousand Islands region, saw the incident as an example of New Yorkers in league with pirates and rebels. Militia were called out, old defences were dusted off, and an armed steamer was sent to cruise among the Thousand Islands. When an American steamer, the *Telegraph*, called in at Brockville, it was challenged by sentries. Getting no response, they fired six cannon shots, three of which slammed into the ship. For a time, trade across the river ceased and nerves were on edge. To show good intent, the governor of New York offered a reward of $500 for Johnston and $250 for each of his men. Border tension eased somewhat after that.

Bill Johnston knew that it was quite unlikely anyone would turn him in. Bold as brass, he wandered at his leisure in Clayton with pistols and knives stuck in his belt. Within two weeks of the *Sir Robert Peel* episode, a letter was carried in several Canadian newspapers. In it, Johnston claimed responsibility for the *Peel* incident, and confirmed that most of his men were Canadians who worked from their Canadian island of Fort Wallace in the Thousand Islands. Fort Wallace, in reality, was a myth. Johnston's headquarters were wherever he happened to be at the time.

During the fall of 1838, the largest rebel society in the United States, called Hunters Lodges, planned attacks on Canada. In mid-November, a late night attack was to have been launched against Prescott. A steamer and two schooners piloted by Bill Johnston approached the Prescott docks. The schooners missed the dock, and turning for a second run at it, ran aground. The Hunters decided to regroup downriver at a prominent windmill, where imaginative spies told them to expect both Americans and Canadian support. That support never came to the windmill, but opposition from Fort Wellington troops and militia did. The rebels were defeated after a pitched battle but not until many lives were lost on both sides.

Bill Johnston slipped back to Ogdensburg at the outset of the Battle of the Windmill. There he managed to attract the attention of the authorities and fled upriver in a small boat. His pursuers caught up to him at an island a few kilometres above Prescott. It was late fall, and the authorities had his boat. Rather than spend a frigid winter without any preparation, Johnston came out of hiding and gave himself up. Falling into the hands of Americans was definitely a better proposition than capture by the Canadians.

After spending a year in an Albany, New York, jail, he escaped and was seldom heard from again. A pirate to some, a folk hero to others, Bill Johnston left his colourful imprint on the Thousand Islands.

Kingston's defences in the 1870s

Cathcart Tower, Cedar Island

THE OREGON CRISIS

Through the mid-1800s, attention was focussed on other frontiers. In the 1840s, American settlers in Oregon claimed a portion of the west coast belonging to Canada. The Oregon Crisis spurred the British government to carry on with its long-delayed plans for upgrading the naval defences at Kingston. Fort Henry had been built as a log blockhouse in 1813 and upgraded considerably over the years, especially in the mid-1830s. To adequately protect the town, shipyard, entrance to the Rideau Canal, and main fort itself, work began on other fortifications.

The type of fortification chosen for six locations was the Martello Tower, inspired by an Italian structure which had stood up to a considerable pounding by British cannon at Cape Mortella, Corsica. Four of these towers were massive, squat, thick-walled, three-storied cylinders. A platform on top supported three cannons, and there were living quarters plus storage on the two lower levels. These four main towers were the Cathcart Redoubt on Cedar Island, a national park island; Fort Frederick on Point Frederick; the Shoal or Victoria Tower at the Kingston Battery in front of the town hall; and the Murney Tower overlooking Lake Ontario from a point on the west edge of the city. The other two towers rise from ditches near the water at Fort Henry. Because the towers were large and complex, and skilled labour was in short supply, the new defences took three years to complete. The Oregon dispute was settled before the construction was finished. Although Kingston's impressive new defences were never put to the test, they stood as solid symbols of commitment to the protection of Canada.

THE
CRISSCROSSED
WAKE

The St. Lawrence is the nineteenth largest river in the world, if one measures the distance from the Atlantic Ocean to the head of Lake Ontario, thereby including all of the Great Lakes as part of the river system. It is one of the world's mightiest rivers and also one of the most difficult to define. Where does it begin? And where does it actually end?

Nautical charts show the St. Lawrence River beginning at the east end of Lake Ontario. The mouth of the St. Lawrence is that imprecise point where its fresh water and current lose themselves to the salt water and tides of the Gulf of St. Lawrence. It could be said that the St. Lawrence flows from the heart of the Thousand Islands, for it is here that the waters of Lake Ontario flood over the Frontenac Arch to begin their oceanward rush. The approximate crest of the Arch is where the Thousand Islands bridge steps from shore to shore across the islands.

Jacques Cartier is credited with naming the river and the gulf into which it flowed in 1535. His arrival in the gulf was on 10 August, the date on the ecclesiastical calender commemorating the martyrdom of Saint Lawrence. In life, Lawrence was a treasurer of the Christian church. It happened in the year A.D. 210 that the leader of the church, Sixtus, was sentenced to death by the Roman emperor, and Lawrence quickly distributed the wealth of the church to the poor so that it would not be taken by the Romans. The emperor was not amused.

NAMING THE ISLANDS

Nearly three centuries after Cartier gave St. Lawrence's name to the river, Capt. William Fitzwilliam Owen of the Royal Navy charted and named the Thousand Islands on the Canadian side of the river. He performed this major task admirably. A glance at the map reveals that the islands generally lie in groups or chains. With his naval background, Owen saw the clusters of islands as fleets of ships or as having other military connection to the War of 1812–14, in which he had taken part.

To the easternmost islands, Owen assigned the name "Brock Group." This commemorates, as does the city of Brockville, Sir Isaac Brock, who gave his life at the Battle of Queenston Heights. Islands of that group are named for contemporaries of Brock and personnel under his command. Grenadier Island honours the fine troops of British regiments. The islands of the Navy Fleet, running offshore west of Ivy Lea, are named for naval officers who distinguished themselves in the War of 1812–14; Mulcaster, Hickey, Cunliffe and Popham are among them. Lake Fleet islands are named for vessels that formed the British fleet on the Great Lakes and Lake Champlain, and include Camelot, Endymion, Bloodletter, Deathdealer, Psyche, Scorpion, Prince Regent, Princess Charlotte and many others. Just off Gananoque is the Admiralty Group, commemorating British Lords of the Admiralty and other senior naval commanders, such as Yorke, Melville and Lindsay. Some names were exceptions to the general rule; English equipment manufacturers had islands named for them. A large number of the islands were left unnamed and as the years went by, they were given names of local or other significance.

SHIPS OF THE ST. LAWRENCE

There is something magic in water. It stirs imagination and emotion in the sailor and shipwright alike. Throughout its history, the St. Lawrence River has been chronicled as the vital waterway of exploration, conquest and commerce of North America. Its story is much more than that of a transportation corridor; it is a study of man and water, exploration and achievement, adventure and invention. The Thousand Islands—granite and green jewels in the river's blue-green setting—focus attention on the river's many facets. The islands and channels demand exploration, and throughout history, man has obeyed the call.

Canoes, of course, were the first craft in the islands, and dugouts

Among the Thousand Islands

were the earliest type, made from logs hollowed out by fire or by laborious work with stone axes. An unknown genius created the bark canoe. It was light, fast and responsive. Bark canoes were the only water transportation used by the French on inland routes for more than fifty years. Canoes have had a longer continuous history on this continent than any type of boat. They still have their place in the Thousand Islands for those who want a closer look at the wildlife of shallows and shores.

The first bateau was brought upriver as part of a show of French military force. To transport such a heavy wooden craft over the rapids between Montreal and Prescott was considered an incredible feat in the mid-1600s. Through the 1700s bateaux were the workhorses of the river. Although long, narrow and open, they could carry as many as five families and their provisions.

Durham boats were similar to bateaux but had a part of the bow decked over and nearly double the carrying capacity. Both craft could sail away from the wind but had to be rowed against the wind because they had no keel to allow them to tack. Thousands of these boats, particularly the bateaux, were built though none survives today. Their usefulness gradually came to an end with the invention of the steamship.

No sooner had the region been settled than lighter rowing-sailing craft appeared on the river. Commonly called gigs, and more delicate and graceful than bateaux, these boats were clinker-built—made of overlapping planks. They were good sailers and rowed easily, carry-

Approaching Brockville, 1800s

ing people and goods swiftly throughout the region.

Heavier sailing craft varying in structure but referred to broadly as schooners made important contributions to the economy during the 1800s, for they permitted cargo and crew to travel the river's deep channels and the Great Lakes. One of the first schooners to skim the Thousand Islands was the *Leeds Trader*, built by Gananoque's founder, Joel Stone.

Although perhaps not a ship in the traditional sense, the timber raft was once a common sight on the St. Lawrence. The first rafts here were assembled in the 1790s of pine and oak cut on the riverbank and islands. Timber rafting was principally a Canadian industry in this region and Canadians even cut timber on the unsettled American shore. Most of the logs were destined for Quebec City, to be loaded aboard ships bound for Great Britain. Some went to local sawmills, where there was a growing demand for building material. At one time, there was a flight of locks built at La Rue Mills to carry logs from the St. Lawrence up to the mill beyond the rapids at the creek mouth. Many rafts were assembled at the mouth of the Gananoque River from trees cut along that river system.

By far the largest timber rafting operation was at Garden Island, just east of Kingston. Hiram Cook and Dilena Dexter Calvin leased a portion of Garden Island in the 1830s to make and forward oak barrel staves. After a few years, the timber forwarding trade became the mainstay of the island business. In the first years, rafts of 200 m³ were sent downstream. Later on, rafts as big as 1400 m³ were forwarded.

THE ST. LAWRENCE RIVER SKIFF

When one thinks of the great distances to be travelled in the Thousand Islands, and the sharp chop of the afternoon waves, rowing does not seem an attractive means of transportation. Yet a remarkable craft—the St. Lawrence River skiff—was built there in the 1860s to respond to the riverman's need. These light, stable, straight-tracking and very fast craft were originally designed to be used as fishing boats, but they quickly became an everyman's craft. They came along in the days when steamers made river transportation practical, but when the steamer was yet too big and costly for most individuals to own.

The skiff was usually rowed, though comparing the St. Lawrence River skiff to other rowing boats is like comparing a tricycle to a ten-speed bicycle. It was also a good sailer. There was no rudder, so the skiff was manoeuvred by shifting one's position to lift, turn or dig the bow and stern, in much the same way as sailboards are handled today. Needless to say, skiff races were exhilarating.

Skiffs were built on both sides of the river. The first one was probably made at the D.A. Bain Boatworks in Clayton, New York, and those of the Andress shop, located first in Gananoque and later at Rockport also became popular. Lengths varied anywhere from 4.27 to 6.70 m, with around 5 m the favourites. A number of these marvelous skiffs are being restored and used today.

The late E. Andress, Rockport, working on his last St. Lawrence River skiff

Fishing from a skiff

Although assembling the rafts was hard work, there could have been few finer pleasures than drifting through the Thousand Islands aboard a raft on a beautiful day. This first part of the journey was relaxed and only the occasional raft went aground on a rock. If such a grounding happened, the heavy, freshly cut oak logs broke free from the pine logs to which they were lashed, and sank. Some of these oak logs can still be found in the river today.

Inventor James Watt in 1769 had developed the steam engine to the stage where it could be used as a power supply, but it was not until 1803, in Scotland, that the first steamer was launched. In 1807–08, Robert Fulton put a British-built engine into the ship the *Clermont* in the Hudson River. John Molson made history at Montreal in 1809 when North America's second steamer, the *Accommodation*, took to the waves with a six-horsepower engine built at Three Rivers, Quebec. In 1816, the *Frontenac*, a schooner-rigged vessel with one funnel, slipped down the ways at the present-day town of Bath on Lake Ontario. The *Frontenac* became the first steamer to ply the upper St. Lawrence and Lake Ontario. Although it was originally intended for use from Prescott to Niagara, the hazard of shoals in the Thousand Islands persuaded the owners to confine the run to the lake waters.

Within a few years more venturesome captains made regular runs in the Thousand Islands, though they found the rapids from Prescott to Montreal difficult to overcome. The steamer *Iroquois* was built in 1832 with the intent of climbing the rapids, but it did not have the needed power. The first runs upstream were made with the assistance of a ''horned breeze''—a tow by oxen. A stagecoach portage was the customary means of bypassing the rapids.

Steam power proved to be the best means yet to travel the Thousand Islands. Sailing ships made slow progress upriver against current and prevailing downriver winds, especially in the narrow channels where currents are swifter and winds more fickle. One of the early steamers to be built in the area was the *William IV* in 1832 in Gananoque. A major shipyard developed on Garden Island, where tugs and specialized timber carriers were built in support of the square timber trade. As time passed, the variety of steam-driven boats steadily grew: cargo carriers, passenger lines, local mill and supply ships, tugs, ferries, tourboats and eventually private yachts travelled the channels of the islands.

The age of steam left its mark on the landscape of the Thousand Islands. Throughout the region, the average age of the older trees is about 100 years. They are the offspring of trees that were cut for fuel as well as timber during the years when wood-fired steam engines

The Frontenac

were at the peak of popularity and created a heavy demand for firewood. Huge stacks of wood marked the busiest steamer landings. Although the trees on most islands were only selectively cut, several islands were set ablaze by sparks from the stacks of passing steamers. Better boilers, fired by coal in larger ships and naphtha in some launches, came along in time to save the forests from a complete change in character. One of the last fuelwood depots to operate on the river was at the store at Darling dock, Darlingside, just east of the Thousands Islands bridge.

During the age of steam, the lasting character of communities developed in the Thousand Islands. Many steamship companies formed to link towns and villages along and across the river, or to provide tours among the islands. Stores, restaurants and hotels were established and prospered because of the summer river traffic.

LIGHTING THE WAY

With an ever-increasing number of ships on the river, there was a corresponding number of shipping mishaps among the innumerable treacherous shoals and shallows in the Thousand Islands. Navigating the channels in broad daylight was difficult, but travel at night was downright hazardous. Merchants in the upper river and Great Lakes found it frustrating to see their goods cross the ocean and be brought past the difficult rapids between Montreal and Prescott only to be damaged or lost when the ships went aground in the islands. Consequently, some communities took it upon themselves in the mid-1800s to build lighthouses on the most dangerous shoals. Governments on both sides of the river constructed gas-lit lighthouses and put them in the care of lightkeepers. On his travels in Canada in 1861, author J.G. Kohl wrote:

> The lighthouses too tended to convey the impression that we were not upon the mighty St. Lawrence, but on the artificial waters of some pleasure-ground—for they were elegant white buildings, like pavilions or kiosks—sometimes half hidden in a grove, sometimes rising from a little island promontory. They are numerous, and of course very necessary, as the winding watery channel is continually changing its direction in this labyrinth of islands.

Some of the earliest lights in the Thousand Islands were at Quebec Point on Wolfe Island, at Aubrey Island, the Spectacles, Redhorse Island and on the Jackstraw Shoal near Gananoque. Others were built at Gananoque Narrows, Lyndoch Island, on the west end of Grenadier Island, at Sunken Rock off Alexandria Bay, at Rock Island (where Pirate Bill Johnston served his sentence) west of Alexandria Bay, and at Cross-over Island west of the Brock Group. Many of the early lights on the Canadian side were built in the mid-1850s. Even with the lighthouses, night travel was still uncertain. Captains who knew the river were guided by the shape of the shore, lights of the towns and familiar farm lanterns.

THE ST. LAWRENCE SEAWAY

It seems ironic that such a hazardous section of the St. Lawrence–Great Lakes waterway could have gone so long without improvements other than lights and markers, yet that is what happened. Rail transportation was getting better, and with the opening of the West, railways were being paid considerable attention. Steamships were a major focus in the river, but it was by rail that many people came to the Thousand Islands in the decades around the turn of the century.

There are two major river passages through the Thousand Islands, harking back thousands of years to the melting of the glaciers when the St. Lawrence was an outlet for two courses. One runs north of Grindstone, Wellesley and Hill islands; the other hugs the American shore and is the deepest and straightest route.

The south channel was the obvious choice to develop as a seaway, and blasting cut the depth of the channel to a minimum of 8.5 m. Buoy and light systems were upgraded. Considerable work had already been done in the Great Lakes to create a shipping channel. On 4 July

Lighthouse, Wolfe Island

1958, the St. Lawrence Seaway was completed, but it was not officially opened until 26 June 1959, when Queen Elizabeth II and President Dwight Eisenhower held ceremonies aboard the Royal yacht *Brittania*. From the time the Seaway was opened to traffic, large ships have been confined to the main channel through this region. Flags from many nations have been carried through the Thousand Islands.

OF RIVER AND ROADWAY
Since the first days of settlement, riverboats were the backbone of the region's transportation system, but the role of boats on a local scale became rapidly less important some twenty years before the Seaway opened. Automobiles were a fact of everyday life in the 1930s. As they improved and their numbers increased, so too rose the demand for roads. Car ferries connected the communities across the river. Indeed, the weekend lineups at the waterfront villages were like social events. It was just a matter of time before the volume of traffic seeking to skirt the east end of Lake Ontario justified the demand for a bridge.

The idea for the bridge was conceived in the early 1920s, but bills permitting its construction were not signed until 1933 in the United States and 1934 in Canada. The choice of location in the islands was easily made, because the narrowest crossing meant the lowest cost and greatest ease of construction. This crossing happened to be at

International goodwill at the opening of Thousand Islands Bridge, 1937

about the centre of the Frontenac Arch and where the channels are narrowest. Piers for the bridge touched down on two national park islands, Georgina and Constance. Construction started early in the spring of 1937, and the five-span bridge was officially opened on 18 August 1938 by Prime Minister William Lyon Mackenzie King and President Franklin Delano Roosevelt. At about the same time, improvements were made to roads along both shores of the river.

Highway traffic to and through the islands soon vastly increased. The greatest impact of the bridge and roads was on the communities on both sides of the river. There was no longer a need for ferry services across the river nor for passenger and freight stops along the shore. The role of these towns as focal points for traffic and trade changed overnight.

The major road on the Canadian side of the river had been old Highway 2, lying well inland from the shore. Local traffic followed the Old River Road, which skirted ridge and river edge. Farmhouses and villages had been built along this road and it was part of a way of life until the 1930s. Then Highway 2S, later renamed the Thousand Islands Parkway, dramatically changed marshes and ridges that beforehand had been considered impassable. Today, the parkway furnishes motorists with an excellent view of the Thousand Islands, and takes the place of the river as the link between communities.

The last steamer, the *Brittanic,* called at Mallorytown Landing in 1938. Trucks and wagons no longer rumbled down the big dock at

Thousand Islands bridge

Mallorytown Landing, nor to other piers in the area, to meet freight shipments. An era of local dependence on the river as a highway was at an end and a new era for travel in the Thousand Islands had begun. Cars replaced trains as the means by which people came to the region, giving tourists an individual mobility never before known. Following World War II, the river has seen ever-increasing recreational boating traffic similar to the steam yacht revolution at the turn of the century.

House of Seven Gables, Himes Island

FROM
THE WALK-AROUND
VERANDAH

Our passage among these (Thousand Islands) was most picturesque; now
wandering through labyrinthine channels scarcely wider than the breadth
of the steamboat, now crossing broad reaches of the river as large as our
English lakes. The grand scale of nature in this country, always striking
. . . The variety of wood, rock, and water is endless, and if the islands,
which are of all dimensions, and considerably exceed one thousand in
number, were not so uniform in height, the scenery would be perfect.
Looking into the future, which in this part of Canada unfolds visions of
boundless prosperity, I thought of the time, probably not far distant, when
these islands will be the summer homes of merchant princes whose fleets
will cover the St. Lawrence.

C.R. Weld, 1855.

There is a broad verandah at the cottage. It wraps around those
sides of the building that offer a view of the river. Even though
its floor is well painted, there is no mistaking a footworn path
among the wicker chairs and past the cushioned settee. Certain chairs
are placed to give the best survey of the river through the spreading
boughs of pine and oak trees. One set of chairs overlooks the channels, making it easy to see who comes and goes and to spot friends
who might be hailed to dock for a chat. Merits of many a sunset have
been discussed from the settee. Each summer brings its little flurry of
events, but on the whole the scene from the verandah scarcely seems
to change from one year to the next.

DEVELOPMENT

One might say that it all began back in 1787 at Merchant's Coffeehouse in New York City. There, Alexander Macomb purchased at a public auction most of upper New York State, including the islands on the American side of the St. Lawrence River. When Macomb's plans for development did not succeed as he wished, the islands again came into the custody of the state. After the War of 1812–14, Col. Elisha Camp of Sacket's Harbor received the patent for these same islands. Twice more the American islands changed hands when in 1845 they were purchased by two businessmen, Azariah Walton and Chesterfield Parsons for $3,000. Parsons dropped out of the picture, and Walton became a partner of the astute businessman Andrew Cornwall of Alexandria Bay. In 1854, a gentleman by the name of Seth Green, who later became Fish Commissioner in the State of New York, approached Cornwall to purchase an island from which he could "study fish." A bit unusual, thought Cornwall, but why not. Green, given his choice of any island, selected Manhattan Island, near Alexandria Bay, paying $40 for it. Thus was sold the first of the Thousand Islands for recreational purposes. Realizing the potential for sales of the islands and developments in Alexandria Bay, the team of Cornwall and Walton set to work. Parts of many islands were cleared of timber and were sold, with the provision that every second island was to remain undeveloped. Those who purchased islands were required to build cottages upon them.

Events followed a somewhat different course on the Canadian side of the river. Lands of the Mississauga Indians in the Thousand Islands were transferred to the Department of Indian Affairs and were put up for sale. In the 1870s, when the steamer made travel in the islands practical, Tremont Park and Hay islands near Gananoque became popular vacation sites. As well, inns along both shores of the river were gaining in popularity. After having vacationed in the islands, many people wished to buy an island for themselves. At about this time, a number of surveys and assessments of the Canadian islands were carried out. Eventually it was decided which ones would be sold, with a value placed on these, and which would remain as government property for lighthouses or other stations. By 1891, only 58 islands had been sold, but these totalled about 1500 ha. The remaining 833 islands on the Canadian side came to just 330 ha.

By the late 1800s, the fame of the St. Lawrence River had spread. A leisurely cruise through the islands and an exhilarating run by steamer down the rapids from Prescott to Montreal was a focus of any visit to this region. George Pullman, inventor of the Pullman car, took an interest in the Thousand Islands project. In 1872, he invited General Grant, who was then running for the presidency of the United States, to his island home. He also approached Andrew Cornwall. "What we want to do, Andrew," he is reported to have said, "is to make much of the General's visit here and it will advertise the islands as no other thing we can do. To have the President of the United States as our guest is quite an honour." As Pullman predicted, more than a little interest in the area was generated by Grant's visit. Investors rushed to build the palatial hotels for which the islands became famous. A flurry of building on the islands took place in the 1880s and 1890s, and indeed some men's homes became their castles. Clayton and Cape Vincent became the railway destinations Pullman suspected they could be, with up to twenty trains a day pulling onto the sidings.

The soaring interest in the Thousand Islands was felt on both sides of the river. Sportsmen found that fishing in the river was excellent. A number of the hotels catered to the angler's interest, and the famous hospitality of this region's vacation industry was born. Experienced rivermen worked from a number of the hotels, leading the fishermen to the secret haunts of bass, pike, walleye and muskellunge. Some hotels had steam launches to tow a string of skiffs into selected areas of the river, thus saving the guides and fishermen the chore of rowing. At noon, the skiffs would congregate at an island for an often sumptuous shore dinner, with fish supplied by the lucky angler. Afternoons would slip by with tale-telling, perhaps a little lie-swapping and usually some good fishing. At dusk, the launch would again collect its string of skiffs for a return to the hotel.

Activities around the hotels kept a fisherman's family occupied, but a favourite pastime was the excursion boat. These craft began a tradition of touring the islands which continues today as a central attraction of a visit here. Searchlight cruises were very popular. The boats would probe the channels and bays at night, highlighting various features with a powerful electric light, or viewing the colourful lanterns hung from verandahs and trees of island homes. Some famous old ships of the day were the *St. Lawrence,* the *Islander,* the *New Island Wanderer* and the *Castanet.*

The Thousand Islands were promoted as an exclusive summer mecca for the rich, as passengers on the excursion boats might well have been inclined to believe. A number of splendid homes were built, especially in the Alexandria Bay area in what came to be known as Millionaire's Row. Most famous of the summer homes was, and remains, Boldt Castle on Heart Island, built in the 1890s by George Boldt, the bellhop who became the millionaire owner of New York's

Thousand Islands Dressing

No book on the Thousand Islands would be complete without a word about Thousand Islands dressing. One day, George Boldt, builder of the renowned Boldt Castle on Heart Island, asked the chef on board his yacht to dress the salad with something a little special. Using a good deal of invention, for there was not much material to work from, the chef did indeed produce a winner. Chopped green pickles in a tangy sauce represented the myriad of islands of which Boldt was so fond. The chef became the famous "Oscar" at Boldt's New York hotel, the Waldorf Astoria, where he introduced Thousand Islands dressing to an international clientele.

For a simple version of Thousand Islands dressing, combine ketchup, mayonnaise and green relish in proportions to your liking. Here is a more sophisticated recipe:

1 cup mayonnaise	1 Tbsp chopped celery
¼ cup tomato relish	5 chopped green olives
1 Tbsp chopped red pepper	1 chopped hard-boiled egg
1 Tbsp chopped green pepper	lemon juice and Tabasco sauce to taste

Waldorf Astoria Hotel. The castle, left incomplete when Boldt's wife died, was the most conspicuous of his endeavours in the Wellesley Island area, which included the building of canals, enormous boat-houses, recreational buildings and a golf course.

More common architecture on the islands were two-storey frame houses, resting on foundations of rough-hewn granite. Each of these is an expression of the owner's, architect's and builder's creativity, but one thing many have in common is the walk-around verandah.

The older cottages in particular have other structures near them that reflect life in the islands. The boathouse, of course, was important. It was often rebuilt to accommodate the owner's interest in boating over the decades. The St. Lawrence skiff was not just a fishing craft; it was the average person's means of getting about the islands. To house it properly, the skiff house was built at the water's edge, with a ramp running into the water from a dry shed. As the years passed and powerboats came along, a dock was added. Most were crib docks of stone-filled log boxes supporting deck timbers. To protect powerboats, drive-in boathouses were built, where boats could be lifted clear of the water for the winter. A spare room or guest house was often built overtop the larger boathouses.

Water supply was another important consideration. Before electricity became available, roaring gasoline-powered motors and pumps were housed near the water's edge in a building of their own. To avoid having to crank up the gas-driven pump too often, cottagers erected water storage tanks at a level above the pumping to allow gravity feed. Some of these tanks were built into the top storey of the cottage; some became elaborate towers in their own right, and others were a simple metal or wood tank on stilts.

Ice houses and woodsheds too were fairly common. Occasionally, honeymoon and guest cottages were built near the main cottage.

Throughout the greater portion of the Thousand Islands, the builder chose the cottage site and character to reflect the lay of the land and its natural features. The contrast of most of these islands to Millionaire's Row is striking, since with the latter, the dwelling dramatically dominates the scene. Each case, of course, was a product of the attitudes of the day. Upon reflection, it could be said that where the richness of the natural scene was lost, a richness in the cultural heritage of the islands was gained.

Church camps were some of the oldest and most substantial developments in the region. Two were established in 1875, one by the Methodist Church at the west end of Wellesley Island, and the other by the Methodist Episcopal Church at the west edge of Brockville. In the early years at the Wellesley Island site, known as Thousand Island Park, campsites were sold or rented and cottages were built in the years that followed. The old Thousand Island Park hotel burned in 1890 but was replaced by the Columbian, reputed to be the best above the city of Montreal. It too burned, in 1912, and with it was lost much of the rest of the Thousand Island Park. A Presbyterian Camp, called Westminster Park, was erected in 1878 on Wellesley Island, facing Alexandria Bay. It had a dock, boarding house, several cottages and long winding drives through the woods.

Another camp worthy of mention was begun in 1881 by the American Canoe Association. Its first meets were at Canoe Point on Grindstone Island. In 1901, the Association purchased Sugar Island, east of Gananoque, where the members' families still camp

There were perhaps three major events that brought the greatest changes to the scene from the verandah viewpoint. The turn of the century saw the heyday of private steam yachts. White hulled and graceful of line, they set the easy pace in the islands. The First World War made fuel difficult to obtain, and many of the launches were turned over to the governments for the war effort. Of those that went into mothballs, many did not emerge following the war, for the internal combustion engine rendered them obsolete. Fortunately, some of the steam launches have been restored to run again.

During the stock market crash of 1929, many wealthy island owners saw their fortunes and property slip from their hands. Homes and hotels closed, some never to reopen as decay or fire took their toll on the wooden structures. Roads and the bridge were built in the Depression, and automobilists used them to advantage in the following years to make quick sightseeing trips in place of the lengthy stays of former days.

Following World War II and the increase in tourism, new resort areas opened across the country, and these became more and more accessible as transportation improved. The Thousand Islands was faced with competition from other scenic attractions. However, in recent decades, the islands have regained much of their popularity. They are known as one of the best cruising grounds and destinations for boaters. Tourboats, fishing guides, hospitable lodges and superb shore dinners continue to represent the renowned character of the Thousand Islands.

Church service on the water at Halfmoon Bay

Vesper services have been held in Halfmoon Bay at the southeast end of Bostwick Island near Gananoque every Sunday in July and August since 1887. Each week a different denomination from Gananoque takes its turn conducting the service. The pulpit, on a cement and stone platform just above water level near the back of the bay, is a granite block. The pews of this singular cathedral are the boats that carry worshippers to the island. Boats tie up to a thin iron rod fixed to the cliffs that form the inside of the bay.

As the name Halfmoon implies, the bay's shape is like that of a crescent moon. The property around the bay was purchased in 1901 by a Boston man named David Wallace, who visited relatives each summer on Bostwick Island. When he died in 1904, Wallace willed the land to the town of Gananoque.

ST. LAWRENCE ISLANDS NATIONAL PARK

St. Lawrence Islands is Canada's fifth oldest national park and was the first in Canada to be created east of the Rocky Mountains. Whereas most national parks are single, substantial land units representing the region in which they occur, St. Lawrence Islands is quite another situation. The park is made up of scattered individual properties, a layout which reflects the circumstances of its origin.

As early as the 1870s, vacationers to the region began to take an ever-increasing interest in purchasing island land, and by the 1880s and '90s, many of the longer and mid-sized islands on both sides of the river were privately owned. (On its side of the boundary, the Canadian government held custody to most of the islands, having received title from the Mississauga Indians; when the land was sold, the proceeds were turned over to the Indians.) Gradually, area residents were being cut off from free access to the islands where for centuries they had hunted, fished, picnicked and cut wood.

In 1874, residents petitioned the federal government to reserve some islands for public use, to no avail. Noting that the United States government had established the world's first national park at Yosemite Valley in 1874, the editor of the Brockville *Recorder* Thadius Leavitt editorialized on 6 September 1877:

> No where on the continent of America, or for that matter in the world, is there a national park of equal beauty and magnitude as the Canadian Thousand Islands. That it should be preserved intact no statesman will hesitate to deny. From Brockville to Kingston our citizens are unanimously in favour of its retention in a state of nature, and we believe that their views will be seconded and upheld by an enlightened and liberal Administration at Ottawa.

Perhaps because there were no national parks in Canada at that time, the suggestion was not acted upon. In the spring of 1904, the residents again petitioned for such a park, supporting their request with the gift of a 1.6-ha piece of property by the Mallory family at Mallorytown Landing. Finally on 20 September 1904, the first nine islands of St. Lawrence Islands National Park were set aside.

The first park islands, those as yet unsold, were near riverfront communities. They included Aubrey, Mermaid, Beaurivage, Camelot, Endymion and Gordon islands in the Gananoque area, Georgina and Constance islands near Ivy Lea, and Adelaide near Mallorytown Landing. In 1905, Stovin Island at Brockville and a parcel of land at the west end of Grenadier Island near Rockport were purchased. That spring, docks and pavilions were constructed and a caretaker from Gananoque was hired.

In 1919, Broder Island at Morrisburg was acquired for the park, but it was one of several islands subsequently submerged in the construction of the St. Lawrence Seaway. The 2 ha parcel at West Grenadier was enlarged to 4 ha in 1924 when lighthouse property was transferred between government departments. Also in 1924, Cedar Island, just off Fort Henry at Kingston, was transferred to the park from the Department of National Defence. The Mallorytown Landing property was enlarged in the 1950s and developed as the park headquarters. As the years passed, a number of other properties were purchased including Milton, Thwartway and Mulcaster islands, a portion of McDonald Island, land on Grenadier, Squaw, Car and Shoe islands, and eighty-two islets and rocks held in trust by the department of Indian Affairs.

During the late 1960s, park planners sought to ensure that the National Park system would represent all natural regions of Canada. St. Lawrence Islands National Park had been created long before any such detailed planning was thought necessary. Even so, a scrutiny of the park revealed that though it was geographically tiny, the region as a whole was rich with natural features of national importance.

Various ideas were developed to deal with the restricted size of the park. During the debate over the park's future, residents of the Thousand Islands began to fear that their properties might be included in an expanded recreation area. But when residents and interest groups of the region entered into a frank, constructive discussion of the role of the national park, a common ground emerged. Not only was there appreciation among the participants for the truly national significance of the region's natural and cultural features but it also became apparent that both the park and the community were an integral part of the fabric of the Thousand Islands.

A VISITOR'S GUIDE

The Thousand Islands lie in the upper St. Lawrence River between Kingston and Brockville. St. Lawrence Islands National Park is a sample of the Thousands Islands. Primarily an island park extending from Cedar Island off Kingston to Stovin Island near Brockville, it includes all or parts of twenty-one islands, some eighty-three rocky islets and shoals, and a mainland area at Mallorytown Landing.

The park headquarters is located at Mallorytown Landing, at the junction of the Thousands Island Parkway and Leeds County Road 5. Leave Highway 401 at interchange 675, and follow signs south on Leeds 5 (Mallorytown Road) to the park. The offices and a campground are on the north side of the parkway; the day-use area is on the south side at the river.

The park islands are accessible only by boat. Those areas with visitor facilities are marked in the park brochure, which is updated regularly. It is available throughout the park and can also be obtained by writing: St. Lawrence Islands National Park, Box 469, R.R. #3, Mallorytown, Ontario K0E 1R0, Canada.

The park is open from Victoria Day weekend, about 24 May, to Thanksgiving weekend in October. During this time, all facilities in all park areas are fully serviced. However, many facilities and programs at the park operate year-round on a more limited scale.

Mallorytown Landing is the park's most developed area, having a campground, picnic area, beach, docks and boat launch, and interpretive exhibits depicting the natural and historical features of the region. The majority of the larger islands in the park have docking, a few primitive-type campsites, wells and privies. A fee is charged for overnight docking. Because of the scattered nature of the islands, there is no way of anticipating where docking space, campsites, or mooring buoys are available. Reservations are not possible; all facilities of the park are open on a first-come, first-served basis.

While Mallorytown Landing is accessible either by automobile or boat, the only way to reach the park islands is by boat. Most visitors to islands travel in their own craft, but there are alternatives. A number of houseboat and sailing yacht charters are available at various ports along the river; several marinas rent small outboard boats by the day. Water taxis are available at marinas and towns.

Tourist information concerning accommodation, restaurants, boat tours and other services is available from the Eastern Ontario Travel Association (located near Ivy Lea at the Thousand Islands Bridge), R.R. #1, Lansdowne, Ontario K0E 1L0, Canada, (613) 659-2188.

Day use area and campground, Mallorytown Landing

Interpretive Programs

The interpretive program of St. Lawrence Islands National Park is designed to help visitors discover the story of the Thousand Islands first hand. It is a year-round service, though the types of programs vary seasonally.

The Visitor Centre at Mallorytown Landing, with exhibits about the region's natural and human history, and a display showing the hulk of a gunboat of the War of 1812–14 era, is open seven days a week during the summer. Also in summer, Parks Canada interpreters present family film and slide shows and children's programs, monitor topical events, and conduct tours at Mallorytown Landing, on the park islands, around the community, and in the area's major campgrounds.

Throughout the school year, there is an in-depth school interpretive program, as well as talks and tours on many weekends for the whole family. A calendar of events is available from the park office. There is no charge for interpretive programs.

Day Tripping

So, you have a few days in the Thousand Islands, and you wonder how to make the most of your time? Here are a few suggestions.

Boat Tours. Take an excursion on a tour boat in the islands. The route taken by each boat line is different, but all offer a chance to explore to the heart of the islands. Be sure to ask the crew to point out

Park naturalist and visitor

highlights along the way. The length of the tour varies, partly because of the distance from the port of origin to the central area of the Thousand Islands. Tours start from Rockport, Ivy Lea and area, Gananoque and Kingston in Ontario, and from Alexandria Bay and Clayton in New York.

Historical Highlights. Because of its long and colourful history it is not surprising that the area supports several museums, heritage houses and fortifications relating to the Thousand Islands. Interesting general subject museums are located at Brockville, Gananoque and Kingston. For insight into military history, visit Fort Wellington National Historic Park at Prescott, Old Fort Henry and Fort Frederick at Kingston, and Sacket's Harbor in New York. Natural history is well portrayed at Kingston's Marine Museum and at the Clayton Shipyard Museum. Bellevue House National Historic Park in Kingston, McDonald House in Gananoque and Springfield House in Escott show visitors an aspect of life in the past century.

The above are but a few examples of historical points of interest. By stopping at an information bureau, or at the park's Visitor Centre, directions can be found to many more historical features.

International Tour. A full day's round-trip driving tour of the Thousand Islands could take the following route:

Starting at Ivy Lea, Ontario, drive to the Thousand Islands Bridge and cross the first main channel of the St. Lawrence River to Hill Island. There, for a small charge, you can ride an elevator to the top of the Skydeck where you will have an excellent overview of the

Thousand Islands. Continuing along, you will cross the granite bridge at the International Rift between Hill and Wellesley islands. After clearing United States customs, you may wish to visit the Minna Anthony Common Nature Centre on Wellesley Island. A second major span of the bridge leaves the island to lift across the main shipping channel to the New York mainland. From there, drive west to Clayton and then to Cape Vincent where a car ferry crosses to Wolfe Island. Another ferry, the *Wolfe Islander*, runs from the north shore of this island to Kingston. Highway 2 to Gananoque intersects the roadway leading from the ferry dock. The Thousand Islands Parkway begins just east of Gananoque, and you can return to Ivy Lea by way of this road.

Be sure to allow plenty of time for this trip, as there are many interesting scenes and features en route. Local guide maps, available from information bureaux, are a definite asset.

Island Adventures. If you have had some boating experience, a day in the islands will be a memorable experience. Several marinas, from Mallorytown Landing to Gananoque, rent open aluminum boats and outboard motors, should you not have your own. Be sure to purchase the appropriate nautical chart; do not hesitate to review it with the marina operator. The chart will help you avoid shoals, and will reveal interesting passages to explore. Use Canadian Hydrographic Services chart 1420 for the Admiralty and Lake Fleet Islands (Gananoque area), chart 1419 for the Navy Fleet Islands and bridge area (Ivy Lea and Rockport areas), and chart 1418 for the Rockport–Grenadier Island–Mallorytown Landing areas.

While most of the islands are privately owned, you can picnic on any of the national park islands.

Area Events. Be sure to stop at the information bureaux in each community to pick up a local calendar of events. There is always something exciting happening in the region.

Camping

There are two types of camping experiences at St. Lawrence Islands National Park: the mainland campground, accessible by automobile, and the island campsites, which can be reached only by boat. All sites are available on a first-come, first-served basis.

The Mallorytown Landing campground is located on the north side of the Thousand Islands Parkway, at the junction with Leeds County Road 5. This campground has sixty-four sites, each with a barbecue and picnic table. There are no hook-ups or showers, but washrooms provide hot and cold running water. A supervised beach, change-

Setting up camp on Camelot Island

house, picnic shelter, playground and the Visitor Centre are located a short walk across the parkway. Also available are a boat launching ramp and both day-use and overnight docking. A self-guided nature trail begins at the northwest corner of the campground.

There are campsites, though in limited numbers, on many of the park islands. Because of the fragile nature of the environment, the sites are usually individual and isolated, having been placed where the least injury will be done to vegetation and soils. McDonald Island and the central area of Grenadier Islands have deeper soils and therefore a larger number of campsites. Island sites are designated by numbered barbecues. Each island has a well, and though the water is tested regularly, it should be boiled as a precaution. Most islands have picnic shelters.

You will find a number of campgrounds on the mainland in the Thousand Islands region. Two of these are provincial parks: at Brown's Bay and Ivy Lea. The majority of the campgrounds in the region are privately operated. At many of these you will find a full range of services, including electricity. Some have pools, small stores and coin-operated laundries. A list of these campgrounds is available from the Eastern Ontario Travel Association.

Only springtime campers in the Thousand Islands will encounter blackflies, and in any case, these are never numerous. Late June and July visitors will meet with mosquitoes, but they are a nuisance only at dusk or in deep shade. Even so, mosquito repellent is a worthwhile purchase.

The Show Boat *at Mermaid Island*

There are no poisonous or dangerous snakes in the region, and no need whatsoever to be concerned about these harmless animals. Garter snakes frequent grassy fields in search of earthworms and insects. Northern water snakes are often seen in the water, and may be attracted to swimmers as they splash about, but they will escape quickly once they learn that people are the cause of the commotion.

Cruising
The Thousand Islands is a yachtsman's paradise, and the park islands are favourite vacation destinations. An island-by-island description of St. Lawrence Islands National Park follows on pages 113-127.

Before setting out for any island or for a cruise, check the nautical charts: shoals and shallows abound. Canadian Hydrographic Services charts numbered 1418, 1419, 1420 and 1421 cover the Canadian sector and most of the United States sector of the Thousand Islands. They are available at most marinas. For those who trailer rather than cruise to the Thousand Islands, there are launching ramps at most marinas and in the waterfront communities.

Those who wish to charter a boat here will find both sailboats and houseboats available. The best advice in this matter is to peruse the directories in boating magazines that pertain to the area, or write to the Eastern Ontario Travel Association for current listings. Book early in the season, as this is a popular cruising area.

Following are a few tips for the cruising boater:

The Thousand Islands, sailors' delight

— Docking space on the park islands is usually at a premium in July and early August, and several islands may have to be visited to find a space.

— Depths at the park docks are not marked on the hydrographic charts, and they give only a vague idea of depth in bays, so be conscious of the draft of your vessel. There is a charge for docking.

— Public docking space is found at the waterfront communities. There may be a charge for the use of these docks.

— Mooring buoys, recognizable by their orange tops and white bottoms, are found at some park islands. There is no fee for the use of these buoys. They are located in water that is deep enough for most keel boats.

— Dinghies may well prove their worth. They are useful if you need to get ashore from an anchorage or if there is no docking space, and they are a good way to explore the island shorelines.

— Anchoring is a good skill to master. There are numerous fine bays in which to drop a hook if you wish a secluded evening, or if dock space is not available. (Charterers should check with their company on this matter.) The bottom is water-weed choked and silty in some places, making it difficult to get a solid purchase with an anchor. This is less a problem in deeper water. When at anchor, the current and wind in some bays may work against each other to send the boat drifting back and forth. To avoid this problem, anchor where there is enough current to hold the boat steady.

– Anchor lights are required overnight at anchor or at moorings, since there is considerable nighttime traffic on the river.

– Mask, snorkel and fins open the underwater world for you. There are many types of aquatic habitats to explore: rock ledges, marsh edges, shallow bays and cliff faces.

– Shoals are a hazard outside of the main channels, but the value of the exploration may be worth the risk. Keep an eye on the charts and watch for glassy calm spots (usually weed beds) and green-brown water (often rocky shoals). White cylindrical buoys with a red band around the middle have been placed by the Thousand Islands Association on many shoals and rocks in well-travelled channels. Remember that most depth finders tell water depths under, not ahead of, the hull, and that depths change rather abruptly in the Thousand Islands.

– Water can be found at pumps on the park islands. This water is regularly tested but as a precaution should be boiled before use. use.

– Mosquitoes are abundant some years, but most appear to feed at about sunset. Close up the boat at dusk to avoid trapping them inside for the night. After it is fully dark, the hordes seem to vanish.

– Marinas in the region are well equipped to handle repair work. Fuel, water and pump-outs are found at most marinas.

– Groceries can be obtained near the docks in Rockport and Ivy Lea, and there are provisions at Mallorytown Landing. In the larger towns, groceries are at a greater distance from the docks. Ice can be purchased near the docks or at marinas in nearly all cases.

Canoeing

Canoeing in the islands can be a rewarding experience, but canoeists should be aware of the sometimes large wake of powerboats and the steep chop on the river. There is a sheltered route through the islands of the Navy and Lake Fleet chains, and in the Admiralty Islands. As well, Landon's Bay and Jones Creek provide interesting exploration. One is advised to bring a canoe to the region; there are few places where they can be rented. Park islands make good destinations on the river, but note that camping is limited to the designated campsites.

Fishing

Fishing is one of the most popular pastimes in the Thousand Islands. Small and largemouth bass, northern pike and perch are the fish most likely to be caught in summer and fall. Many fishermen came to the islands in the fall to try their luck on muskellunge, which lurk along

Canoeing the islands

the shoals, venturing forth infrequently to feed. The world record "muskie," weighing 31.72 kg, was caught just south of Gananoque on the Forty Acre Shoal. Ice fishing too is popular, northern pike and perch being the usual catch. Each spring, fishermen line the marshy banks of the river at dusk to catch brown bullheads. Those new to the river, or who wish to fish in expert company, will find it worthwhile to team up with a fishing guide.

Regulations and seasons vary slightly from year to year. Information on this, and licensing, is available at tackle shops and marinas throughout the region, or from the Ministry of Natural Resources, Oxford Avenue, Box 605, Brockville, Ontario K6V 5Y8.

Photography

There is a great deal to capture on film in the Thousand Islands. Here are a few suggestions:

Mornings will give you the best conditions, especially for scenic and close-up photography. In fair weather in summer, clouds develop and humidity increases after noon so that the the blue sky loses some of its intensity. As well, winds pick up as the day progresses. There is considerable glare off the water at midday. You may wish to put your camera aside during that time to save your film for the colour, shadows and highlights of mornings and evenings. Cloudy and even rainy days often give the best conditions for photographs in the forest. Contrast from light to dark is less extreme, and colours seem more

Skiers on the Nordic Trail

brilliant on film. Film and processing is readily available in the region.

Bicycling
Although there are no pathways specifically for bicycles, mainland touring prospects are good. Be conscious, however, of your visibility in this hilly terrain. The Thousand Islands Parkway parallels the river. Highway 2, while it has narrow shoulders, is also an east-west route. Less travelled are the county and township roads, and of these, the road from Rockport to Escott is especially scenic.

Winter Travels
January, February and the first half of March are the months to explore the winter world of the Thousand Islands.

There are cross-country ski trails just east of Rockport (the Nordic Ski Trails) and at Brown's Bay. Elsewhere on the mainland, the land is privately owned; permission should be gained before crossing it.

Travel across the river, whether by ski or snowmobile, is safe in many places in midwinter. However, local knowledge of conditions and routes should be sought before venturing onto the ice. Grenadier Island is a popular destination. At central Grenadier, a picnic shelter is closed in for the winter, and firewood is provided.

In national parks, the natural environment is protected. The purpose of the park is to preserve this special place in Canada for all time. To this end, please do not pick wildflowers or gather wood for fires. Pets are welcome, but must be leashed and under control at all times. Do not hack or deface trees with axes or knives, as infection and rot will set in at those places. Lines, whether for supporting tents or securing boats, must not be tied to trees; otherwise bark could be damaged or trees uprooted. To help prevent erosion please use the trails provided. The rules for the park are designed to ensure that future visitors will have an experience in the islands that is no less enjoyable than your own.

If there is an emergency on the islands, or should you require assistance, contact a park warden. Use Channel 16 ''Parks Canada Warden'' on the VHF radio, or call the park office from the mainland at 923-5261.

A TOUR OF PARK ISLANDS
Here is a brief sketch of some of the islands:

Cedar

Cedar Island; Kingston in background

This westernmost park island is located just off historic Kingston. It is the last granite island on the west side of the Frontenac Arch. A defence tower, called the Cathcart Redoubt, was built on Cedar Island in 1847 to bolster the defences of Kingston and the Rideau Canal during the Oregon Crisis. The island boasts a view of Fort Henry and some of the other Martello towers. The southwest half of the island was cleared when the Cathcart Redoubt was built, and the regrowth of vegetation there is an interesting contrast to the other less heavily cut northeast end.

Cedar Island is popular for picnics and camping. The docks, though not large, are sheltered from the waves of Lake Ontario. As on all of the islands described here, there is a well with a pump.

Milton

Slender, wedge-shaped Milton Island lies 5 km east of Kingston, near the western entrance to the Bateau Channel. The substance of much of its rugged shores is quartzite which hosts a brilliant orange lichen. Milton Island has a colourful hue, especially in early morning and evening light. There is a small, well-sheltered bay at the east end of the island, and a picnic shelter with a good view of the river.

Aubrey

Aubrey Island lies on the western edge of the rugged granite Frontenac Arch, at a point where it noticeably begins its gentle dip beneath the much younger sedimentary rock. Stunted and bent red oaks on the windswept west shore contrast with a lofty canopy of oaks gracing the island's sheltered centre. Aubrey forms a windbreak for many of the other islands in the Admiralty Group.

One of the many lighthouses in the region stood on Aubrey Island's south bluffs. Look for the remains of it near the orange day mark. Along the path between the two main docks, a depression in the ground indicates the foundation of the lightkeeper's house.

There is a good deepwater dock on Aubrey's east side, a sheltered bay with docks on the south side, and two main picnic areas plus campsites on the island.

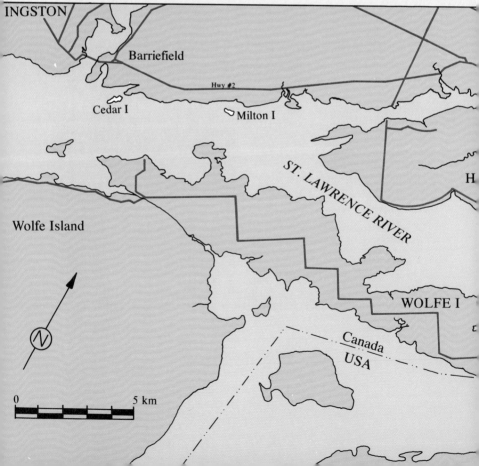

Mermaid

Brute forces of the last ice age left their mark on Mermaid Island. Rounded, polished granite shows where the massive ice sheet laden with rock and debris bulldozed and gouged the stone. The entire island is a near-classic "roche moutonnée"—a whaleback of smoothed rock, broken at the west, where grinding ice pulled loose rock away in its

Mermaid and Aubrey islands (Bostwick Island in foreground)

passing. Look for the big northern water snakes which usually sun on the rocks of the island's west end. Please do not harm them. Like all animals and plants of the park, they are protected.

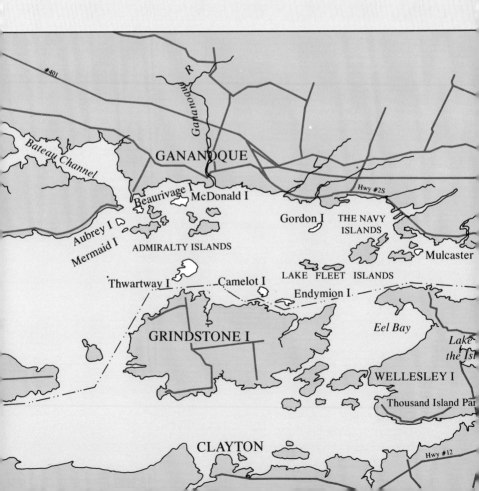

Park Facilities

SERVICES	CEDAR	MILTON	AUBREY	MERMAID	BEAURIVAGE	McDONALD	THWARTWAY	CAMELOT	ENDYMION	GORDON	MULCASTER	GEORGINA	CONSTANCE	W GRENADIER	S GRENADIER	N GRENADIER	ADELAIDE	MALLORYTOWN	STOVIN
Picnicking	⊓	⊓	⊓	⊓	⊓	⊓		⊓	⊓	⊓	⊓	⊓	⊓	⊓	⊓	⊓	⊓	⊓	⊓
Camping	∧	∧	∧		∧	∧		∧	∧	∧	∧	∧	∧		∧		∧	∧	
Shelter	∩	∩	∩		∩	∩		∩	∩	∩		∩	∩	∩		∩	∩	∩	∩
Toilets	🚽	🚽	🚽	🚽	🚽	🚽		🚽	🚽	🚽	🚽	🚽	🚽	🚽	🚽	🚽	🚽	🚽	🚽
Potable Water	🚰	🚰	🚰		🚰	🚰		🚰	🚰	🚰	🚰	🚰	🚰	🚰	🚰	🚰	🚰	🚰	🚰
Docking	⛵	⛵	⛵	⛵	⛵	⛵		⛵	⛵	⛵	⛵	⛵	⛵	⛵	⛵	⛵	⛵	⛵	⛵
Mooring						⚓		⚓								⚓			
Beach						🏊									🏊		🏊		

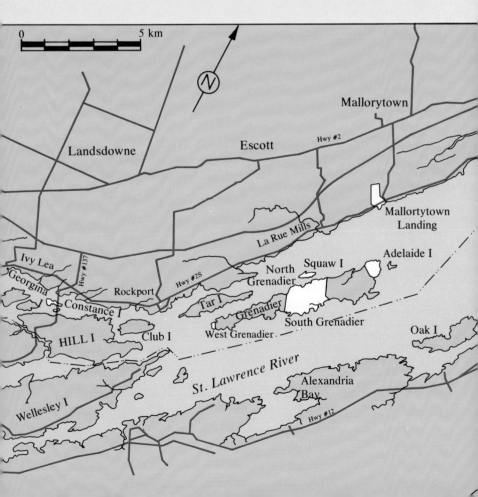

Beaurivage

Its name means "beautiful shore" and Beaurivage has been popular with picnickers and campers for more than a century. Until relatively recent times Beaurivage was actually two islands. As this area is still slowly rising, an aftereffect of the glaciers' heavy burden, a shallow

neck has emerged to join the two higher points of land. Today, deposits from current-carried sand and decaying vegetation accelerate the growth of the young land bridge.

There are a number of campsites, picnic areas and short floating docks at Beaurivage. A crib dock will be found on the northwest end of the island and another more sheltered one in a deep bay on the east side. Anchoring offshore on the east side is good, but be sure to use an anchor light here at night.

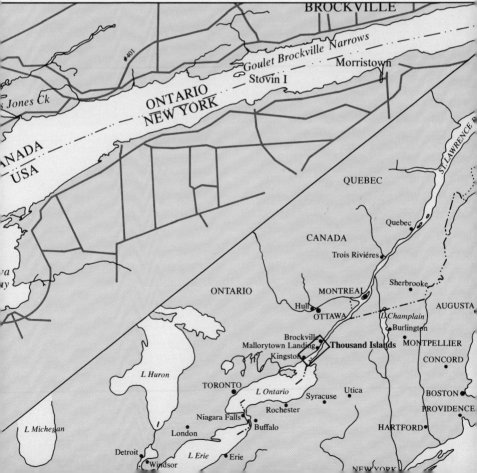

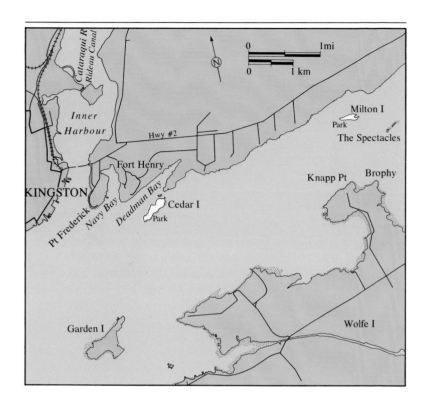

McDonald

Deep soils, a rarity in the Thousand Islands, cover much of McDonald Island. As a result of its relatively level surface, it has a varied history. In World War II it was the site of a Sea Cadet camp. It was later named Rotary Island for the club of the same name. A number of private cottages still remain on the east end of the island. A walk through the forest of today provides insight into past land uses. Tall, old oaks and white pines with few mid-size trees beneath them show that the forest understory was once completely cleared away. In other places there are large clearings.

Ideal for family camping, McDonald has several shady campsites and ample docking space.

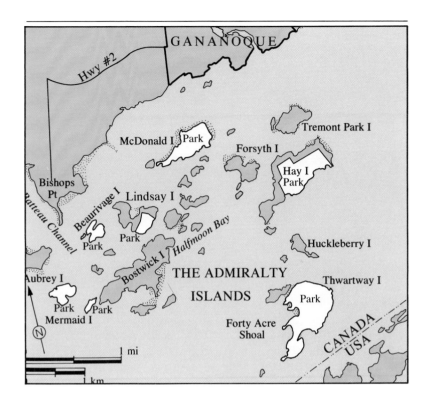

Thwartway

Thwartway is a well-treed wildlife refuge having forest vegetation typical of the region. Rocky outcrops interspersed with pockets of clay form the basic groundwork for a forest of red and white oak, pine, basswood and the rare pitch pine. Mammal life is typical of small islands in the region: hairy-tail moles, voles, short-tailed shrews and little brown bats, to name a few.

A sandy but boulder-strewn west bay is popular with swimmers, and a sheltered south-facing bay makes a good overnight anchorage.

Endymion

Pockets of soil among dramatic rock outcrops make Endymion Island a study in contrasts and habitats. This island is one of the many Thousand Islands whose names commemorate the ships, captains and admirals of the 1812–14 War. In this case, a gunboat serving in the British Navy is honoured.

The deep water of both Camelot and Endymion make them popular with larger boats having deeper draft, but each has only a few campsites because of the rugged landscape.

Camelot

Rugged Camelot Island demonstrates well the fragility of nature where only thin soil covers rock outcrops. The island is generally quite open because of the quantity of bare rock exposed, so slow is the process of soil formation, and so easily is it washed away. Like Beaurivage, the island is divided by a deep valley. But here the soil is deeper and high beech trees tower over a luxuriant trillium patch.

Good docking exists on the east side of the island, and there is a picnic shelter in the valley. Anchoring is very good in a bay on the southwest shore, and off a point on the northeast. Please be aware of the fragility of the island: use the trails and avoid tying boats to trees.

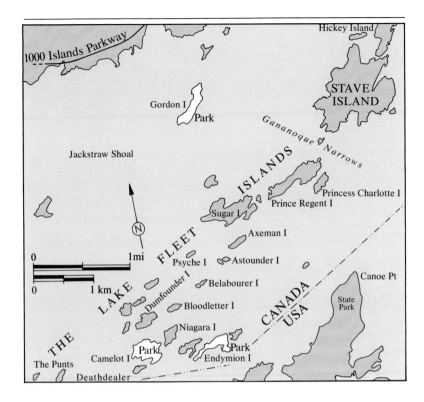

Gordon

Unlike the majority of the Thousand Islands which are granite, Gordon Island is covered by a thin sandstone veneer. This rock is some half billion years younger than that of most other islands. Interestingly, there is a large, round granite boulder near the main dock that was left there when the last glacier melted, and its composition is twice as old as the surface rock surrounding it.

Gordon is one of the richest of the Thousand Islands in numbers of plant species.

There are camping areas at both ends of the island. Since Gordon lies apart from other islands, the docks on both the south and north shores are only partially sheltered.

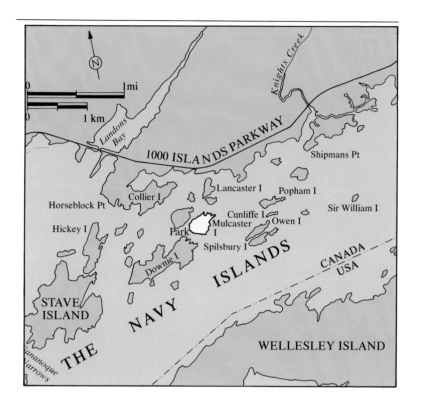

Mulcaster

The rich forest of Mulcaster creates a pleasant atmosphere for quiet strolling. Several large poplars lie along the north shore where beaver felled them. The island is often visited by larger bird species: ruffed grouse, birds of prey and pileated wood-peckers.

There is a limited number of campsites. The sheltered docks are popular and fill early in the day.

Map labels:
Rockport
HWY #137
1000 ISLANDS PARKWAY
CLUB ISLAND
vy Lea
Ivy Lea Park RAFT NARROWS
Georgina I Park
Lost Channel
Constance I
Wallace I
Thousand Islands Bridge
HILL ISLAND Park
Park
Park
Park
CANADA USA
WELLESLEY ISLAND
U.S. #81
LAKE OF THE ISLES
N
0 1 mi
0 1 km

Georgina

Georgina and its neighbouring islands lie approximately at the centre of the Frontenac Arch, where the tightly clustered islands confine the channels and form a nearly complete barrier to eastern Lake Ontario. Here the lake actually begins its tumbling descent to the sea. The river swirls through narrow channels to plunge into a deep pool east of the island group.

Georgina and Constance islands

Because of the rugged terrain, there are a limited number of campsites. The docks are well protected from wind, but there is noise from the bridge overhead, and the main channel is busy throughout the day.

123

Hiker on Georgina Island

Constance

Like nearby islands, Constance has such irregular topography that the climate over short distances and on a small scale is noticeably altered. Sun-warmed, dry, breezy south-facing slopes contrast with cooler, moist, protected northeast slopes. Such distinct differences produce dramatic changes in vegetation patterns.

This is a small island with limited facilities but with an enjoyable setting. The bridge passes overhead of the island.

Grenadier West

Larger islands tend to host a greater variety of plant and animal life. This is reflected at West Grenadier, the westernmost tip of Grenadier Island. Three species of pine—red, white and pitch—the southern fragrant sumac, and one of two locations in Canada for deerberry distinguish this tiny property.

Docking includes two crib docks, one with deep water and a second in shallower water. There are two picnic shelters, one of which was built in 1905, a year after the park was established.

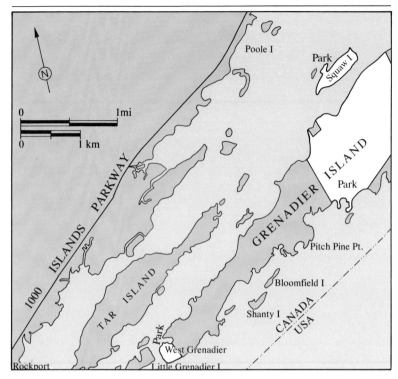

Grenadier North

North Grenadier is on the north-central portion of Grenadier Island. The area, now low and flat, was flooded and levelled by the flowing waters of melting glaciers. It was ideally suited for the farming that began in Loyalist days. A well-known lodge, Angler's Hotel, once stood at the picnic site, but was long ago destroyed in a fire. The windmill stand was situated in front of the hotel. Beware of the rocks from the old crib dock; a few are still north of today's floating dock.

Grenadier South

Also part of the Central Grenadier property, South Grenadier is a well-serviced park area. It is an open site, having once been a farm field. A township road runs through the north section of this property, and is a good means to explore from one end of the island to the other.

There are a large number of campsites, two picnic shelters, a washroom with hot and cold running water, a small beach, and a long dock with several finger docks. One of the picnic shelters is closed in for use during winter months.

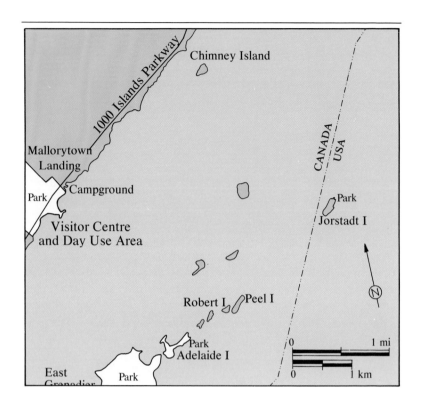

Adelaide

Adelaide is actually three small islands connected by sandbars overgrown with cattails and alders. Long ago, there was an Indian campsite on the island, probably because of the good fishing in the area.

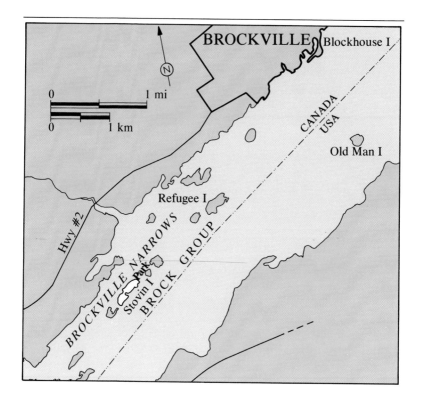

Stovin

The easternmost of the park islands, Stovin lies at the edge of the Frontenac Arch and offers a dramatic view of the St. Lawrence Seaway. Huge ships pass within metres of the island's shores. Stovin was well polished by glaciers; look for glacial grooves where boulders were dragged by the ice.

Camping, picnicking and docking are located on the island's south side, away from the seaway channel.

CHIMNEY ISLAND

There are many Chimney Islands on the St. Lawrence River. One of them lies just offshore about 3 km east of Mallorytown Landing.

In the fall of 1799, two Métis hunters built a small hut on the island. They were joined in midwinter by a French Canadian who immediately set about building a log house, cutting trees on the mainland and dragging them across the frozen river to the island. The newcomer left early in the spring, but returned soon by bateau with lime from Kingston to make mortar for a large chimney which he built at the log house. Again he left, returning in May with a bateau full of household goods. He was accompanied by a very pretty woman of white and Indian ancestry, who was apparently his bride. The couple took up residence on the island, entertaining visitors but otherwise keeping to themselves. No one knew who they were or anything of their means of support.

In the fall of that same year, Enoch Mallory and Joseph Bark were hunting when they noticed that the island was aflame. Hurrying there they found the French-Canadian at the shore in a half-burned canoe, his skull split by a tomahawk. There was no trace of the woman.

Thomas Sherwood, magistrate at what is now Brockville, investigated but found no clues to the murder. The two Métis hunters could not help since they were away from the Thousand Islands region at the time. And if they knew of the murdered man's identity, they were not inclined to reveal it. Rumours flew, but the mystery was never solved.

During the War of 1812–14, Chimney Island was one of the many staging points for British canoe and bateau convoys on the St. Lawrence. Convoy crews could rest there under the protection of local militia.

A blockhouse was built on the island just a few months before the war ended. Although its defences totalled only four cannons and thirty-five men, the blockhouse had a good location: it overlooked the channel along the north shore; larger ships had to pass within a few hundred metres of it; and there was deep anchorage at the island's east end. The mainland shore was only a short distance across the shallows and the little blockhouse could not be cut off, yet surprise from land would be difficult. Three gunboats patrolled among the islands, on the alert for American ambushes.

The blockhouse drew criticism from its troops for its lack of comforts. It was cold and drafty, and the chimney smoked terribly. Quite likely the stones used for that chimney were those of the unknown Frenchman's cabin. The blockhouse chimney fell long ago but a later owner of the island had it rebuilt and it still stands as a prominent landmark on the river.

CREDITS

All photographs in this book have been provided by Parks Canada.

Illustrations on pages 46, 52, 53, 59, 67, 80 and 81 are courtesy of Provincial Archives of Canada; on page 70 , courtesy of the Royal Ontario Museum; and on page 85, courtesy of 1000 Islands Shipyard Museum, Clayton, N.Y.

Maps are based on Canadian Hydrographic Service charts 1977-79. These maps are not to be used for navigation.

READING LIST

Banfield, A.W.F. *The Mammals of Canada.* Toronto: University of Toronto Press, 1974.

Chapman, J.L. and Putnam, D.F. *The Physiography of Southern Ontario.* Toronto: University of Toronto Press, 1966.

Godfrey, W. Earl. *The Birds of Canada.* Ottawa: National Museums of Canada, Bulletin No. 203, 1966.

Guillet, Edwin C. *Early Life in Upper Canada.* Toronto: University of Toronto Press, 1933.

Hosie, R.C. *Native Trees of Canada.* 8th ed. Toronto: Fitzhenry & Whiteside, 1979.

Leavitt, Thaddeus W.H. *History of Leeds and Grenville Ontar from 1749 to 1879.* Belleville, Ont.: Mika Silkscreening, 1972.

Mika, Nick and Mika, Helma. *United Empire Loyalists: Pioneers of Upper Canada.* Belleville, Ont.: Mika Publishing Co., 1976.

Parsons, Harry. *Foul and Loathesome Creatures.* Ottawa: Parks Canada, Dept. of Supply and Services, 1976.

Preston, Richard A. and Lamontagne, Leopold. *Royal Fort Frontenac.* Toronto: University of Toronto Press, 1958.

Rowe, J.S. *Forest Regions of Canada.* Ottawa: Information Canada, Publication No. 1300, 1972.

Scott, W.B. and Crossman, E.J. *Freshwater Fishes of Canada.* Ottawa: Fisheries Research Board of Canada, Bulletin 184, 1973.

Soper, J.H. and Heimburger, M.L. *Shrubs of Ontario.* Ottawa: The Royal Ontario Museum, 1982.

Wright, J.V. *Ontario Prehistory, an Eleven-Thousand Year Archaeological Outline.* Ottawa: National Museums of Canada, 1972.

Note: Booklets and brochures describing all of Parks Canada's National Parks, National Historic Parks and Heritage Canals are available free from Parks Canada, Information Services, 10 Wellington Street, Hull, Quebec K1A 1G2.

INDEX

Canadä